BIBLICAL KEYS
TO A
SUCCESSFUL
DIVORCE, MARRIAGE
AND BLENDED FAMILY

BIBLICAL KEYS
TO A
SUCCESSFUL
DIVORCE, MARRIAGE
AND BLENDED FAMILY

A Handbook for Couples, Pastors, Counselors, and Small Groups

DOTTIE KLEIN

CITI OF
BOOKS

CITIOFBOOKS, INC.
3736 Eubank NE Suite A1
Albuquerque, NM 87111-3579
www.citiofbooks.com
Hotline: 1 (877) 389-2759
Fax: 1 (505) 930-7244

Ordering Information:

Quantity sales. Special discounts are available on quantity purchases by corporations, associations, and others. For details, contact the publisher at the address above.

Printed in the United States of America.
ISBN-13:   Softcover   978-1-963209-52-5

               eBook   978-1-963209-53-2

Library of Congress Control Number: 2024901747

Table of Contents

Foreword...i

Introduction... iii

Chapter 1: Marriage 1

Chapter 2: Divorce Counseling...13

Chapter 3: What Effective Parenting Looks Like 22

Chapter 4: How to Begin Again with Someone New!—Dating.......34

Chapter 5: Long-Term Relationships.................................45

Chapter 6: The Role of the Husband.................................57

Chapter 7: The Role of the Wife..68

Chapter 8: Remarriage of Empty Nesters 76

Chapter 9: Rooted in Dysfunction 85

References : 92

About The Author : 93

Foreword

It's about time someone addresses one of the biggest problems people are having not only in the country but also in our American churches. Marriages, divorce, children, and even blended families are Dottie's subjects. She approaches these giant problems with simple and practical ideas that can be applied by any of us. Describing the problem is one thing, but having "the answer" is another, and Reverend Dottie Klein hits the nail on the head with each chapter of great wisdom.

Everyone should read this book even if you already have a great marriage because we need to keep our marriages strong, for they are always under attack. You will also inevitably run across people who need directions in their life, and, if you're prepared, you may be the one who points the way for their healthy future.

Hope you enjoy this book as much as I did. I think you will.

Pastor Jim Cobrae Founding
Pastor of The Rock Church and
World Outreach Center
San Bernardino, California

Introduction

This book is intended to provide the building blocks needed in a kind of reconstruction plan for redecorating one's life. From the beginning of Creation, God designed the family unit to provide a safe place for parents and their children, including the privacy of a sexual union between husband and wife. In the security of the home, a husband and wife have the freedom to breathe freely and share honestly and openly with each other.

I believe the high divorce rate in our country is the reason why we see a continual decline in the number of couples getting married, choosing instead to cohabit, testing the waters to make sure the relationship will work. Unfortunately, as we will see later, cohabiting often creates the complete opposite result the couple is seeking.

It is easy to obtain a divorce these days; however, divorce only creates problems, and cohabitation is certainly not void of complications either. Foolishly, couples live together not realizing that, and by so doing, there is no protection against legal consequences and other unseen dangers.

God designed marriage to include celebration and commitment by publicly stating promises to each other in the form of a vow. This way, as a unit, we can move freely, openly, and honestly with each other.

On the flip side, when cohabiting, if one or both parties feel a sense of insecurity, it would be impossible to have freedom in their relationship. Important interaction cannot freely express itself if you are always afraid your live-in partner will, one day, walk away. However, although I strongly oppose divorce, when abuse is involved, divorce does offer security for the children and the spouse. Unfortunately, in most cases, those who benefit the most in divorce court are the attorneys.

To illustrate this more clearly, several years ago, my husband, Dan, and I were vacationing on a cruise where, every evening, there was live entertainment in the theater. Because Dan was detained, I went ahead to get us a good seat close to the stage and took a seat next to a young man who was saving a seat for his wife also. As we began to converse, I learned they were on their honeymoon. I congratulated him and told him my husband and I were ministers and that we conducted premarriage classes for couples before we married them.

He said, "You are the perfect person to ask this question. My wife and I lived together for several years and were getting along well, so we decided to get married. Now, we seem to be having all kinds of arguments in areas we never seemed to disagree before, why is that?"

I answered his question by saying, "Marriage is the only safe, secure place a couple can truly be honest with each other, and when you were living together, issues would arise as well as conflict. These issues would, normally, have been addressed during the courtship period of your relationship, but because you were living together, and your sexual union was not secure, fear caused those issues not to be addressed."

"Couples do not realize that when they live together, they create an insecure bond. They tell their friends and family about their arrangement and do not want to face embarrassment if the choice they made does not work out. This is constantly in the back of their minds.

"Instinctively, we know living together is not right. When conflict arises, fear that the other person will leave or end the relationship is always in the back of their minds. After all, by living together, you are both financially committed to the very same overhead without the security of marriage. Simply put, you both were not being honest with each other when you chose to cohabit.

"When conflict reared its ugly head, your fear of losing the other person did not allow you to address the issues. Your lack of having made a secure, lifetime commitment before God did not allow you to face these problems or personality differences with direct attention, but instead, they got pushed out of the way and were left unresolved!"

By getting married, your sexual union is protected by marriage and commitment, creating a safer haven where you can address these conflicts honestly. Living together and uniting in a sexual union before marriage is, therefore, a deception.

Courtship, on the other hand, is a very important part of a relationship. In that arena, a couple learns about each other by seeing their partner in as many situations and circumstances as possible. "There is no topic that should not be discussed. Finances, family, children, future goals, expectations, individual wants and dislikes—the list goes on and on. All these need to be resolved before a couple even considers sexual activity." We will touch on this in chapter 3.

"Courtship allows a couple to view each other in as many situations as possible, to really know if they can adjust to each other's differences in marriage and face serious issues head-on without the fear of losing what the other person is contributing to their live-in arrangement or having to save face if the arrangement doesn't work.

"It is important that a strong friendship be developed long before sexual intimacy takes place in the bond of marriage. This is what God intended for the security of the family unit. However, in a culture that is used to *instant gratification*, asking a couple to practice *delayed gratification*, in the form of *celibacy*, requires a lot of self-discipline. Ideally, if this would occur, divorce would not be as prevalent as it is today."

As I explained these things to this agreeable young man, he could see what was happening inside his new marriage relationship. I often wonder where that couple is today and if their marriage survived. Statistics tell us, couples who live together before marriage have an 80 percent chance of failure. Is it any wonder our children get lost in the mix?

Marriage is a partnership. Simply put, no one in business would ever think of opening a business with a partner without a contract. In business, you do a market analysis and a business plan. You carefully plan your expectations and strategy for the future success of your business, with the hope that it will provide security for you and your partner for a long time, maybe even for future generations. Marriage is no different. It needs a contract, a commitment, and a plan with goals for the future.

My husband, Dan, and I began our journey on July 7, 1979. We both endured marriages that ended in divorce, and each had children from those previous marriages. At the time, no one was available to prepare us for this journey. The divorce rate in the '70s was 3.5 to every one thousand marriages. It's a pretty low percentage compared to today's five hundred out of every one thousand (50 percent). For every two marriages, there is one divorce.

The main example we could learn from was a 1970s sitcom called *The Brady Bunch* where, as I recall, there were no visitation or child support issues or past spouses that brought conflict into their marriage unit. From all indications, their pasts were over and not a part of the present or future. Therefore, from all appearances, life was just day-to-day encounters easily handled, unlike most second marriages today that face overwhelming conflict right from the beginning of unification.

My husband, Dan, had been married ten years to his high school sweetheart. They married and had their first child within the first year of marriage. Because his wife contracted measles in the first trimester of pregnancy, little Danny was born with many birth defects. He was blind, had a heart defect, and when he was eleven months old, they both were told he would never be able to be educated. The doctors performed many surgeries on his eyes and heart. They told Dan and his wife to have another child as soon as possible. Kenny was born the same year as little Danny.

As their beginning years progressed, the stress of having a handicapped child took its toll on Dan's wife; and when little Danny was just three years old, she suffocated him.

Dan was working when he got the emergency call. His son had stopped breathing, and by the time he met the ambulance leaving their home, it was too late. Both parents were in their early twenties. Dan was called upon to give an account of why little Danny had so many scars on his body. It was when he left the office, leaving the door slightly open, he overheard the doctorand the coroner's conversation. It was then he found out his wife had suffocated the child. However, both officials agreed pressing charges would not bring positive results given the age of the parents. Not the best choice. After many years, Dan realized she must have had a mental breakdown.

As a result, for years, Maureen could not live with her choice and drank to deal with her pain. This destroyed what was left of a marriage and a young second child's life. She embezzled money from a doctor who she was working for and spent time in jail for that. Shortly after their divorce, Maureen quickly remarried and had several more children while Kenny remained the subject of ongoing custody pursuits.

When Dan and I met and married, Kenny was fifteen years old. He was a teenager with a lot of problems. He had left home and was living with a cousin in Northern California. He was also drinking, using drugs, and not doing well in school. Neither Dan nor I were aware of the extent of these problems at the time we began blending our family. My former marriage relationship began at a young age. We met in our high school years and married in February following our graduation. We were rooted in strong family values, and children were not thought of or planned for until my first husband completed his college education, at least that was the plan. I worked and put Steve through college. Our first child was born in the middle of his junior year of college. Both of us were able to continue working until he completed all four years and got his degree in education. We went on to have our second child when my first child, Chris, was almost three.

Steve and I had a very happy marriage and relationship up until our twelfth anniversary. At that time, Steve's grandfather died, and his mother sent him a plane ticket to come to Pittsburgh for the funeral. It was that short interruption in our lives when our marriage relationship changed abruptly. The next five years our marriage went into a downhill spiral, and I did not know why.

I did not know that Steve had begun to explore an alternative lifestyle and learned later that he became a homosexual. It took me a while to discover as he was never upfront with what was happening. In fact, he said I was the problem because I had become so deep into my Christian faith, and because he now had a master's degree, I was not intellectually compatible with him anymore.

Our marriage came to an end with me taking custody of our two children. We never had a formal visitation agreement. Steve lived only a few miles away, and the children were free to see him whenever necessary. My children were young teenagers when the divorce was final in 1976. Making us married just a few months shy of seventeen years. Our settlement was not a battle; in fact, Steve and I worked things out smoothly. The children, however, used their father as leverage and would often contact him as a go-between for our disagreements and dysfunctional moments.

It took several years before I was able to balance a career, family, and dating life. Not sure I ever got it right, but somehow, I managed to meet a man who introduced me to an opportunity to pursue a career as a sales representative in the Christian book and gift industry. It was important to me, after my failed marriage, that I find a man who loved the Lord as much as I did and have a marriage centered on Christian values.

During those single years, I dated but never found the right person until Dan and I met. Both of us had reached a point where we were very ready for a permanent relationship. After just five short months, we made our relationship a full-time arrangement and combined our lives bringing three children into the mix when we married.

As I write this now, we must have been very optimistic. We certainly had no idea what we were doing. We did not even counsel or get an ounce of advice. We jumped in with all we had to offer, and this book is the core of what we learned the hard way—from personal experience!

Since then, God has guided us to help other couples blend their families. Our marriage has never once reached a crossroad where divorce was an option. We were dedicated to our God and knew we were not going to allow anything to come between the foundation of our marriage. Yes, we made mistakes. We picked ourselves up and kept on going. There is no formula here. No blueprint with calculated perfect outcomes.

Each blended family has many different twists and turns. There are many common threads, but each family fabric is uniquely woven together, and success is the result when a couple is committed to each other—the primary key to achieving their desired outcome.

INTRODUCTION:

1. Second Marriage after divorce or death of a spouse carries with it a very high-risk factor. Currently_____fail rate.

2. Because of this fail rate couples choose to cohabitate. Testing the water to see if it works first. However, if these Couples do enter into marriage the statistics are even higher_____fail rate.

3. Some of the reasons for failure are:

    a. Bi-passing_____by getting involved sexually before marriage.

    b. Lack of_____discipline.

    c. No_____with past relationships.

    d. Lack of preparedness of the_____for a new step-parent.

4. What are some of the reasons for God's family design in the first place?

    a. Provide a_____place.

    b. Open_____with honesty.

    c. Privacy and security for_____ _____.

5. The divorce rate currently is: for every_____marriages there is_____divorce.

6. Marriage is_____fold._____,_____and_____.

    We must have agreement in all three areas not just one Or two,

    _____will be the outcome.

    How can two walk together unless they agree? Amos 3:3.

ANSWERS:

1. 70%

2. 80%

3. a. Courtship; b. Self; c. Preparation; d. Children

4. a. Safe; b. Communication; c. Sexual intimacy

5. Two, one

6. 3, Body, mind, spirit, failure

The following principles are foundational not only to a blended family but also to any family. These principles are not, in some respects, new or unusual, just rarely followed. I believe that the reason why divorce is so high in our society, and in faith-based homes and families as well, is that these simple truths have been ignored. It is my hope that by uncovering the forgotten, age-old principles discussed herein, we will, ultimately, change the future of the family unit.

Chapter 1

Marriage

Purpose. Honor the union between a man and a woman as foundational

The first miracle Jesus performed was at a marriage celebration. Marriage is a very important union. It is the source and foundation of a healthy family unit. God designed marriage to be the foundation of *truth* and *self-worth* for all mankind. Because marriage is one of God's highest priorities, I am placing it first on my list for blending a family. From the beginning, God intended relationships to grow together in the bond of marriage. Marriage is the plan for the protection of both parties in all areas of life legally, physically, and spiritually. In the bonds of marriage, a couple has security and freedom. The very first statement a pastor or person officiating a marriage union says to the couple, "Marriage is an honorable estate." It's a brief statement but powerful. What does it mean?

— *First, marriage is honorable to God,* who is the one who authored and founded marriage. When He created Adam and Eve and gave them life and commanded them to multiply and fill the earth, His intention was to use the security of marriage to form a family where each could function in a role that created a strong, protective environment for their children. This was the original plan from the beginning before sin entered the equation. Adam and Eve had a daily relationship with God. The couple honored God from the beginning, and God blessed them.

— Second, marriage is *honorable to our father and mother*. Personally, I was privileged to be a part of a solid home where my parents were married for fifty-four years. Divorce was a disgrace to the entire family in the generation in which I was brought up. It was considered the height of failure and worse than any other life failure. To shack up with someone outside of the bonds of marriage was not even considered. Why? Because it would disgrace our parents. And that included the entire family.

— *Third*, marriage is *honorable to our children* yet to come or, if this is a second marriage, to those living at the time of the union. Why is this important to them? Because marriage is a secure place to create future children and a secure place for raising them. As a couple, you are honoring your children by offering security to them where they can grow and be nurtured. You are giving them peace and a soft place to fall that is away from outside influences that oppose Godly ways. We honor our children by allowing marriage to create safety and protection inside a loving secure environment.

— *Fourth*, marriage is *honorable to future generations*. Marriage is giving them hope. Hope they can look back on and reflect on. Hope when they come to life's complexities that will assure them, with God's help, they can get through it.

— More than all the above influences, *marriage is honorable to the couple*, giving testimony of their love and commitment to each other inside the bonds of their commitment. Lifting each other in high honor after choosing them, above all others, to be your life partner. Saying to all present, "This is my life partner." Giving her the same family name and becoming one flesh is a celebration of love and commitment to each other.

Adam states in Genesis 2:23 (NKJV), "This is now bone of my bones and flesh of my flesh." Genesis 2:25 says, "And they were both naked, the man and his wife, and were not ashamed. It is important for us to leave our father and mother and *cleave* only to each other. No one (neither father nor mother) should be involved in a couple's personal lives unless they have something to do with providing a solution. And never without both husband and wife's knowledge.

In every aspect of a committed relationship, a couple is meant to be one—united and bonded together. This statement could not be clearer, "They were not ashamed of their bodies being revealed to each other." More than physical, they were unashamed to be completely open with each other *body*, *mind*, and *spirit*.

Unashamed! From this statement it is very clear that any time we move outside the bond of marriage and open ourselves up to someone other than our husband or wife, *honor is disgraced*, *privacy and trust are betrayed*, and *there is shame* in that connection. However, we've learned to nullify the shame by *surrounding ourselves with other couples also living together outside the bond of marriage. Knowing others are doing it also lessens the shame.*

Sadly, couples of this generation will come together long before a commitment ceremony of marriage unification. They will live together, share household expenses, and even have children, all without marriage unification. All without honor. These relationships are becoming more and more prevalent in our society today. All they seem to produce is destruction of all parties involved. Most, if not all, are products of brokenness themselves, searching for better answers to well-established questions. They seem to want to break free from foundational truths and traditional beliefs, dismissing them as old-fashioned because they look like they don't work, justifying their reasoning for not entering a unification of marriage by a celebration. Unfortunately, all this creates is *further insecurities* for all persons involved. The future prospect for these kinds of unifications can only produce *destruction, fragmentation,* and *brokenness.* Certainly, in all other areas of life, business, or partnership agreements, we would not even consider starting a transaction without a legal document stating what the *expectation* and *allocations* of the arranged unification will be, holding each party accountable to the agreed standards committed to. Yet the union of marriage is not important enough to be held to the same standard. How is this even possible? What God has given us, intended as His highest priority, we have dismissed as unimportant and not necessary.

My husband, Dan, and I taught premarriage classes in every area where we have lived that included some of the valuable lessons we learned from having to blend our own family. Resources on *how to blend two families* were not available at the time, so we learned through hard, painful experiences, caused by our own mistakes and by the mistakes of others. While we cannot say, "Look at us, we did everything right!" we can say with certainty, "Here are some things we recommend, and here are some things we know do not work." Let me start by telling you about one mistake shared by two couples we counseled:

John and Alex

One evening, when we were teaching our premarriage class, one of the couples, John and Alex, stayed until everyone had left. We sensed they were serious about their marriage working so well that it would set an example to others. They had set their wedding date and wanted Dan to perform the wedding celebration.

It was the first night of our thirteen-week premarriage class, *A Biblical Portrait of Marriage* by Bruce Wilkinson. The lesson was on sexual purity (living a pure life before God) and was very straightforward and convicting. Both John and Alex took it very seriously. To this point, they both had been living together in the same house. The children were old enough to be aware of their relationship. The children were Alex's children from a former marriage. John had no children, and this would be his first marriage. He was living with Alex and her children.

They both said they wanted to do what was honoring to God but were unsure how to do it. I asked if there was any way they could live separately until their wedding date. Alex said John had no place to go; however, she could stay with her dad. They both agreed that was a great solution.

I counseled them as follows: Since her children would be involved in this decision, they first had to agree that they both had been sinning before God, were not setting a good example for the children, confess they were wrong, turn from that sin, and ask God to bless their relationship going forward.

Then, they should take one more step and ask the children to forgive them for disobeying God for not being a good example to them and then explain their plans for future living arrangements. When they left that evening, they moved forward with a plan in place. Both continued the rest of the premarriage classes. They also completed their wedding plans. All of this was done while Alex stayed with her father.

The wedding day arrived, and Dan performed the ceremony in the backyard of Alex's home. It was a lovely celebration. As they were showered with rice and sent on their way to their honeymoon, we were confident they were headed for a secure future. The next morning, we received a phone call from them. Both were in tears. They were tears of joy as they explained to us what their first night together as husband and wife was like; they had never touched each other before. It was as if God had wiped the past completely from their lives. All things were made new. What joy they experienced. God loves it when we are obedient to His will and His Word. He stands only to bless us.

The victory here is, John and Alex have now been married for over twenty years.

Their children are out of the nest and living lives of their own. The big victory for us came when they also applied some of the principles in chapters yet to come, which resulted in the children's father (Alex's first husband) and his new wife coming to church one Sunday morning and giving their lives to Christ.

When we are obedient to God and faithful to apply His will to our lives, the only path for us is His blessings and abundance.

Robert and Joan

Walking in a manner pleasing to the Lord was the topic of teaching and discussion for our home fellowship group. We were going through 1 and 2 Thessalonians. The key scriptures used were based on 1 Thessalonians 4 and were paraphrased in the lesson:

> Finally, brothers we instructed you on how-to live to please God, as in fact you are doing. Now, we urge you in the Lord Jesus, to do this more and more. It is God's Will that you be sanctified; that you avoid sexual immorality; that each of you learn to control his own body. In a way that is holy and honorable, not in passionate lust like the heathen, who do not know God. For God did not call us to

be impure, but to live a holy life… He who rejects this instruction does not reject man, but God, who gives us His Holy Spirit.

Like the early church adding to their number, we too were adding new people to our small group. It was customary for us to introduce new couples to the group by asking them to tell us about themselves and then have each attendee introduce themselves to the new couple. One such couple was still in the dating stage of their relationship. Robert had been in our group for several years. We had grown very fond of him, and we were all thrilled when he found a lovely Christian girlfriend, Joan. Their relationship was progressing into a "love connection," and we fully expected them to, one day, come together in marriage. Joan had only been in our small home fellowship for several months before this evening.

When the introductions came first to Robert, who introduced himself and told where he lived in our community and how long he had attended our church, he told some interesting things about himself, and then we moved on to Joan. She opened by saying she used to live in another part of our community, but she had just recently moved in with Robert! She told us where she was working, and we continued around the circle.

As leaders, we had never been confronted with this obvious display of inappropriate Christian behavior. As leaders and teachers, we had never experienced this before; so in an effort not to embarrass anyone, we just continued with our study. God, however, had other plans as our study that evening was on the above-said verses of scripture— living a pure life in every way before God. We went into the study in a normal fashion, answered the questions in our booklet, had a healthy discussion, and ended our evening in refreshments and prayer. The group was very sensitive to what Robert and Joan had openly admitted, but God in His Word did not leave much room for misunderstanding. The verses were and are very clear in their instruction.

The next day, we received an email from Robert and Joan. "We will not be attending small group any longer as we do not like being singled out!" Looking back on the evening, no one in our group had singled them out. It was God's Word that is "sharper than a two-edged sword" that caused them to feel pricked in their own hearts. I answered them in love.

> We are so sorry you felt singled out. Not one person had prior knowledge of your recent living arrangement. Only God knew and He loves you both so much that He chose this very lesson to help you understand how we are to honor God with our lives. We hope you will reconsider.

As a couple, Dan and I are committed to always walk in love. Our next step was to go to Robert and try to help him see how important it is to walk in obedience to the will of God, but he was not receptive at all.

We then went to our pastor and left it up to the church to handle it further. Our paths never seemed to cross after that Sunday evening. They attended a later service on Sunday, and because Dan and I taught a premarriage class on Saturday afternoon, we went to church Saturday nights. We did not see Robert and Joan for almost a year.

One afternoon, we were sitting at home in our living room when we received a phone call from the pastor's office. Our pastor spoke with Dan telling him Robert and Joan were in his office and wanted to come to our home to speak with us about attending our premarriage class and for us to perform their marriage ceremony. We told him, "Of course, our home is open to them," and they came by that afternoon.

After welcoming them warmly, they told us, not long after the evening when they felt offended, they were each convicted in their hearts to not continue living together. Both had had very hard former marriage breakups and thought they were doing the right thing by living together first (a very common but erroneous thinking these days). But desiring to make the Lord the center of their union, they realized living together was not right and returned to their own houses while continuing to attend all thirteen classes.

Every class was a new adventure for them, and almost without exception, after each class, they would say, "If only we had had this teaching before our first marriages, we would have done so many things differently!"

The blessing was all ours. As we stood before our congregation and their many friends and guests uniting them in marriage, it was indeed a triumphant, Lord-glorifying moment—proving by the testimony of their lives how great our heavenly Father is and how much He blesses us when we are willing to walk in His will.

Summary

Honoring marriage is the number one key toward a couple's success for blending a family. But if you are reading this book, and you are still between relationships—perhaps still married to your children's parent or either going through the process or still deciding what to do—I would stop, take a deep breath, and ask yourself these questions:

1. Did I do all I could to save this marriage?
2. Will my children be better off if we get a divorce?
3. Did I get counseling and take all the steps necessary before jumping out of marriage?
4. Did my partner and I really honor to the above extent my marriage commitment to God, family, and each other?

If you cannot give a loud shout of yes to these questions, I will be the first to tell you that your next relationship and future will not bring you happiness but continued defeat and failure.

How do I know this? As a teacher, pastor, and leader, I have witnessed it time and time again. I want you to do one thing for me. I want you to take your child or children in your arms, then ask yourself how important is their future to you.

Broken homes produce children who easily fall prey to drug addiction, sexual promiscuity, low achievement, and low self- worth. The decision you make as parents today determine their future. How you go about it and your continued interaction with each other going forward will also determine their future. When either one of you walks out of this family unit, you are not only shaping your spouse's future, but you are also reshaping your children's lives.

Children learn what they live. Therefore, for your future and the future of those you impact, please do whatever it takes to work through your present relationship. Then, if you can't find resolve, work out a co-parenting relationship that works for all parties involved.

Finally, do not leave your children in the hands of the court system. I will explain this in later chapters. Be committed to the responsibility of parenting your children. All children deserve to be loved and nurtured by both parents.

When I was single after my divorce, I attended a Christian singles group at the Crystal Cathedral in Orange, California. That night, the topic was "Children of Divorce." The panel consisted of three children from divorced families. Each was a different age. One was eleven, one was fifteen, and one was an adult in her twenties.

Each explained their positions at the time their parents divorced. All were very open about their feelings. They described their lives before the divorce and after the divorce, and we were given the opportunity to ask questions to each of the children. There were many common threads in their testimonies.

Each felt somehow *responsible* or at *fault*, each felt *helpless* to fix it, and each felt completely *out of control* of their own lives going forward, helpless to control their future both economically and emotionally. Each had different transitions, but the impact was the same.

One very common thread each child said struck me deeply. They all said, they fantasize that someday their parents would get back together. Realizing the impossibility of this being a reality, it still was in their thought process. So I pray that you'll see how important it is, for their sake, to make sure you have done all you can to repair your present relationship. When you walk out the door, you must feel no regret or guilt, knowing you tried and have complete peace that you have done your best for the future of your children.

Note. If there are safety issues in your present marriage such as violence or abuse, then you must seek *safety first*. Allow those in authority to bring counsel to the situation. Let the professionals assist you moving forward.

In closing, we honor God when we choose to follow His design for our lives, and because we honor Him, He *blesses us* with *safety, prosperity,* and *peace* in our relationships. Obstacles and challenges will come (that's a fact of life); but for the person who seeks out God's instructions, obeys them, and puts them into practice in daily life, God promises to walk with that person and guide them to "Green pastures beside still waters."

Chapter 1 MARRIAGE

1. _____honor the union of marriage as_____.

2. God designed marriage to be_____of _____and_____.

3. The plan includes_____of both parties involved,_____,_____and

   _____.

4. Marriage provides_____and

   _____.

5. Marriage is an "Honorable Estate."

   a. Honorable to_____, foundational.

   b. Honorable to_____ and_____.

   c. Honorable to_____yet to come, or if second marriage already here.

   d. Honorable to future_____._____they can reflect on.

6. Most important Marriage is honorable to the_____

   _____. A_____of their_____and

   _____to each other.

7. Adam and Eve were "Unashamed " to be completely open with each other. When we move outside the bond of marriage we open ourselves to_____. Privacy and

   _____are betrayed.

8. What is pleasing to God? 1 Thes. 4

   How to live a life pleasing to God?

   a. _____set yourselves apart from the world.

   b. Avoid_____.

   c. Avoid_____. Do not act as if you do not know God.

   d. God did not call us to be_____.

9. He who rejects this instruction does not reject_____but

   _____who gives us His_____.

10. Honoring marriage is the number one key for_____
    in_____.

    If you feel comfortable: Share with the group where you are either in your present relationship or marriage and how you left your last relationship if applicable. If you have children describe your relationship now and what you would like it to be.

    Note to leader: At this point allow open sharing and discussion within the group. This will give insight into where each person is in the group and areas where wisdom can strengthen each person. Do not force people to be open but you can encourage them to feel comfortable. Try to get them to express their attitude toward marriage before reading the material and their understanding after reading this first chapter .

    In closing: We_____God when we_____
    to follow His_____for our_____.

    _____,_____,and_____come

    from_____to God!

Answers:

1. Purpose, foundational

2. foundation, truth, self-worth

3. protection, legally, physically, Spiritually

4. security, freedom

5. a. God b. mother father c. children d. generations

6. couple, testimony, love, commitment

7. disgrace, trust

8. a. Sanctified b. sexual immorality c. passionate lust d. impure

9. man, God, His Holy Spirit

10. success, marriage, Final statement answers. honor, chose, design, lives, safety, prosperity, peace, obedience

Chapter 2

Divorce Counseling

Unfortunately, divorce counseling is something few couples engage in before obtaining a divorce. In this chapter, let's look at how critical this step is to the future health and welfare of the couple and their children. By not taking this step, divorce can lead to many consequences that would take volumes to contain.

Most of us look for cookie-cutter solutions for solving life's inconveniences, trying to contain the inevitable, only to find it soon crumbles into thousands of destructive pieces. To a concerned parent, divorce counseling is critical for every part of the family's future, including a child's health and mental well- being.

Finding a qualified counselor is perhaps something new to most of us. Knowing there are charges and fees involved usually stops us from pursuing this important step as well as our own perception of what takes place at these sessions.

A good place to begin this process is with clergy in whom you trust. It could also be a couple like us or friends who have already gone through a divorce and could give you wise advice from what they have learned. It is my hope this book will be a good starting point for many couples.

Once you reach this point in your journey (the point of no reconciliation) you have both concluded, the marriage part of your relationship is over, and the future is a great unknown. Bitterness, resentment, and anger all need to be resolved and laid aside to move forward. This must be the first step a good counselor should start with.

When a marriage reaches the point where everyone is unwilling to work on salvaging the relationship, then it is clear the marriage is over. It may take some work to get to this place, but the primary focus needs to no longer be on the couple but, rather, on the future and well-being of their children.

This step is critical to the success and future ongoing relationship the couple will continue to have with their children as all are moving forward. If this step is not finalized and resolved by some degree of peace, it will only create continual battlegrounds, and those who suffer the consequences will be the children.

Considering how 40 to 50 percent of marriages end in divorce, that number increases when couples enter relationships too soon after a breakup or even during a breakup. *For example*: Consider a marriage relationship ending too quickly because a husband is having an affair. The family is thrown into what I call a "violent conclusion." Anger mounts quickly, and the entire family, including extended family, is thrown into complete malfunction.

Nothing is resolved in these types of situations, and the children's lives are completely disrupted. Anger complicates the circumstances while future security and financial concerns, in addition to custody battles, become the focus, putting mental health and financial security at very high risk. Emotions are raw and vulnerable, and, in these circumstances, all individuals involved often make rash choices. In these situations, divorce counseling can help tremendously yet, sadly, usually never takes place.

The partner having the affair quickly enters another marriage that has a 97 percent failure rate. Often the couple decides to just live together, and when this happens, many of those relationships never result in marriage at all. This creates fragmented individuals and is destructive to not only the children but also the entire family unit.

Because of just this kind of destruction, I can't emphasize enough the importance of ending one relationship before beginning another. Therefore, divorce counseling is critical to the future of everyone involved.

There are multiple reasons couples decide to end their marriages.

- Lack of commitment
- Communication—unable to solve issues
- Unfair division of labor in the marriage
- Physical or emotional abuse
- Addiction
- Lack of preparation for the challenge of marriage
- Financial problems
- Sexual issues

The list is as complicated as personalities and people are. It can also include health issues and/ or health issues of children. In addition, we must include the death of a child as well. This pain can often drive a couple apart and destroy a relationship. Getting professional help during this critical time is a *must-do*.

Next is where experience has taught me a valuable lesson (not advice). The trouble in my marriage was not something obvious. We had what I would have characterized as a very normal marriage. We had disagreements and arguments mostly over money or the lack of it from time to time. However, we always seemed to be able to rise above and handle our differences. Until I was blindsided by a left-field standoff or ambush.

My husband, Steve, had gone back to Pittsburgh for his grandfather's funeral. Our children and I were unable to attend due to the expense of airfare. When he returned, he was a totally changed man. It was as if he went from one person to a completely different person when he returned home.

A week or so after his return, I found him sitting in our living room staring off in deep thought. I entered the room and sat down to ask him, "Since you have been back, you seem to be somewhere else. You have not communicated with me at all. What is wrong?" I was in no way prepared for his return response.

"I don't think I love you anymore. As far as this Jesus Christ stuff (our newfound faith in Christ), you can take it and shove it! I am going to go have a good time, and I refuse to end up like my parents." After collecting myself, I asked him what that means for me and our children. Well, he explained he did not want a divorce right now, but he needed time and space to find himself, and he expected me to do the same. He wanted to be free to explore who he was and expected everything to continue as it was. He wanted time to *figure it out*, and I was supposed to go along with this idea.

Forty years ago, considering divorce was a disgrace and total admission of failure, I was in no hurry to rush right out and start the divorce action immediately. In fact, from that moment to the divorce court took almost six years. Adding all the other combined years totaled just two months shy of eighteen years of marriage.

In those six years, there were many moments of pain, compounded by not knowing what the problem was. I was told by Steve I was too religious for him, and now that he had his master's degree, I was not intellectually up to his level and standards of his new friends. He began to have friendships with same sex individuals only, meeting them and sometimes not coming home until the wee hours of the morning or not at all.

I was very suspicious but did not want to give in to my obvious suspicion. In the early seventies, little was ever spoken of homosexuality or the habits of homosexuals. One who was of that persuasion kept it to himself, and his lifestyle was kept in secret, certainly not exposed to normal circles of social society. Therefore, in my own naive state, I would block those thoughts from even entering my thought process, which, perhaps, is why it took me so long to figure out where my marriage was headed.

For some reason, I could not wrap my head around the fact that someone who was homosexual could also have a normal heterosexual marriage and/or relationship. It took me a while to figure out where I was going and how soon!

During that time, I sought counsel from my pastor. He was patient with me. It was indeed painful as well as a very spiritual time of growth for me. I did not rush out to find a replacement to find solace with. I learned how to trust in God in those growing years. It was a bittersweet time as you may have guessed.

I was told by my pastor to take 1 Corinthians 7 to heart. Stand on that statement of scripture that says, "When an unbeliever departs, let them depart," and I being the believer was then free to leave. The unbeliever's action was the only way I could truly be free to move on in my life. I stood on that segment of scripture.

In the last year we were together, Steve moved in and out three times. The third was the last, and it was then I knew divorce was coming, and I fully understood the reason why. I also understood why it took a full six years and the importance of God's timetable. My children would not have handled it sooner nor would I have been able to handle the financial aspect. I did not realize it then. Only the passing of time reveals these things to us. Wisdom and growing through difficult circumstances give us perspective and understanding not found in rushing!

Looking back helps us see how we arrived in this future spot where we are today, whereas, when we are in the moment, we have no idea where we are going or where we will end up. All I can say is, "I know In Whom I have believed and fully trusted God for the outcome of my life." I am glad I did not rush into divorce. I waited for God's time. I sought counsel, but not divorce counseling. To save you, my readers, from some of the grief I went through, I am hoping you will seek divorce counsel.

What Will Divorce Counsel Do?

For the couple

Divorce counseling will give the couple an opportunity to resolve their conflicts and bring them to a point of release. Sorting through the conflict may not dissolve the conflict, but it will help the couple sort through it and come to a point of dealing with the anger and emotion involved in the conflict, taking responsibility for the how, when, and why the situation happened in the first place.

Seeing how and why it happened often gives way to understanding and a place of forgiveness—or at least a point of *letting go* of all the pent-up anger, leveling the field of conflict to finding a workable plan for the benefit of the children going forward. It was a plan that must include the following:

- Peace, safety
- Financial security
- Access to both parents
- Emotional grace
- Proper division of assets
- Equitable interaction
- All family including extended members

In other words, divorce counsel will help in working out most possible foreseen conflicts that may come down the road. Obviously, no one can magically resolve unforeseen things, but we must create a platform to come back together for future problems, designing a workable path forward.

For the children

Without a doubt, children must be the most important consideration in this negotiation. Their safety and financial security *must* always be top priority. Having adult supervision and proper care in the absence of one or both parents is also very important.

Children may suffer a loss of friendships and economic transition due to financial restrictions. Extended family may be involved as one parent may have to move back into their parent's home for a season until a regrouping or continuing education may occur, which would bring about many additional transitional adjustments. These are just a few reasons why the couple's top priority must always be providing stability for the children.

It is also important that the couple understand—they are divorcing each other, not the entire family. Their children will always be their children. No matter what the future brings, the children will always remain in their place on the family tree, so to speak.

The extended family must also be involved in this transition because there needs to be an understanding of how each member must be on board for the welfare of the children, including attitudes and conversations, especially when grandparents are involved in the daily care of the minor children. Negative input from extended family can cause many emotional problems for children and their development. Therefore, consider including parents in divorce counseling.

In conclusion, I can't stress more passionately this important step in the family's interest. Skipping this step could mean the difference between life and death of your child or children at the very most and/ or success in their future relationships. To be heard and wanted, some children struggle to find peace by making poor choices, which can include drugs, alcohol, and sex. No fit parent desires this for the future of their child. To bury a child because of any addiction or, at the worst, suicide goes beyond words.

We must all take heart here and stop the conflict. Take responsibility and time to construct a plan to create a peaceful loving environment in which a child can come full circle, making healthy choices for himself with the constructive input of both parents who are not bickering and fighting over emotional or financial issues. This takes a plan and the help of an experienced objective counselor with insight and wise judgment.

Finally, avoid laying your children and family at the mercy of the legal and court system. Experience has taught us: It will not lead to a positive outcome. Instead, lean on an experienced divorce counselor whose wisdom can oftentimes provide alternative solutions that benefit all parties involved.

Chapter 2 Divorce Counseling

If a couple has reached a point of no reconciliation :

1. _____,_____and_____all need to be resolved or laid aside in order to move forward.

2. God's timing is crucial at this point: Seek individual _____at this point to reach a forward vision for _____ _____.

3. What will Divorce Counseling do?

   a. Give couple opportunity to_____ _____ with an objective third person.

   b. Sorting through_____.

   c. Take hold and accept your_____for the demise of your marriage.

   d. Reach an_____.

   e. Let go of your_____.

4. Reaching a point of_____leveling the playing field to achieve a_____foundation going forward.

5. What are some of the ingredients the plan must include:

   a. _____and safety.

   b. _____security.

   c. _____to both parents.

   d. _____grace and_____.

   e. Fair division of_____.

   f. _____interaction.

   g. _____including extended family must be on board.

6. Children must be the primary concern:

   a. _____and safety when either parent is not available to the child/children.

7. Make a list of adjustments a major move would entail for each one of your children. Take time to consider their feelings.

8. Also consider the impact on family issues.

    a. Grandparents

    b. Extended family

9. We must stop the_____. Stop for the future of your children is the_____you will pay!!!

10. Remove the future of your family from the _____

    _____.

ANSWERS:

1. Bitterness, resentment, anger

2. counseling, God's timing.

3. a. resolve conflict b. major issues c. responsibility d. understanding e. anger

4. letting go, workable.

5. a. Peace b. Financial c. Access d. Emotional, forgiveness e. assets f. Equitable. g. All family

6. Supervision

7. List

8. List a & b

9. conflict, price

10. legal system

Chapter 3

What Effective Parenting Looks Like

I would like to begin this chapter with the "Dear Annie" column I read in my newspaper, the *Villages Daily Sun*, today. Although this was perfect timing for me, as you read this letter, it may sound a little extreme compared to the reason for your marriage break up as well as the behaviors exhibited, but the consequences and the impact on each person are the same when we do not resolve issues before moving on.

Dear Annie,

> I want to know why people think it is OK to harass and abuse other people. My ex brought his girlfriend home, and they spent the night in the garage when we were still married and took our five-year-old daughter out on his dates with the girlfriend.
>
> Then, he abused and harassed me for a year to get me to abandon the house and my daughter so he wouldn't have to pay child support.
>
> During this ordeal, I was ripped off by my lawyer who knew my ex was harassing me and did nothing. My ex and this girl are not together anymore, but I later found out the girlfriend was hitting my

daughter on her hands to punish her when she did something wrong.

I just don't get why there are horrible people in the world who do awful things and don't think they've done anything wrong. Then, have them turn the situation on you, acting as if you deserve it.

After all this, I'm done with men. I don't even date. It ain't worth it. I talk with people on chat sites, and they tell me they don't date for the same reason. Being alone, in this day and age, is just a better way to go. I feel so broken and empty inside, no one would want me anyway. I am ruined and no one seems to care. So, I just want to know why?

Someone who wants to know why?

Although we do not have all the information from this distraught broken woman, I believe I can give my readers a classic illustration of what not to do when making future plans. This letter is a perfect illustration of a couple who never worked through their issues. I would like to begin with the ex.

From the information given, the scenario is an all too familiar one. Let's call this husband, Randy. Randy met and married his wife, and together, they had a little girl. Given the age of their child, we know they were married at least five or six years— considering pregnancy, it could have been as long as seven years.

Randy, statistically, was in a very vulnerable time in most marriages as seven to eight years is when couples often begin to develop conflicts in their relationship. Often, husbands come home from work, and their wives, who also work these days, are focused on their child, getting dinner, and the responsibilities of taking care of household duties. Depending on the example they were shown from their own parents, some husbands do not adjust well to this rhythm and fail to get involved in the process, placing themselves in front of the TV or using activities, friendships, or hobbies to stay "out of the way."

Some fathers understand how to be a father, but there are those who feel they have no reason to participate in the joint experience with their wives and say, "I will wait until the child is older when we can have more interaction."

Likewise, women, depending how they were raised, take over food prep, children, and household responsibilities, pushing their husbands out of the picture. Men feel completely left out, so they're off to their hobby in the garage or the neighbors for a beer—leaving wife and child to their usual routine. Day after day, week after week, loneliness creeps into the relationship. Randy is easy to figure out. First, I have witnessed, time and again, how people tend to repeat patterns in their lives. The following is a list of things I can clearly find without knowing Randy personally.

1. He has no purpose or structural boundaries.
2. He moves totally without thought of the long-term consequences.
3. He took no leadership in his relationship with his wife.
4. His needs and desires are the most important goal for him.
5. He has never been taught or led by example. (He might have come from a broken home.)
6. He has no connection with God.

Without leadership growing up, he is unable to express himself, and it appears he fell into a pattern of already seeking another before ending one relationship. Without too much thought, he probably began his relationship with his wife the same way. I may refer to Randy in the next chapter on dating and courtship.

It is easy to conclude that Randy and (let's call her Becky) Becky entered a physical sexual union before any foundational wisdom was gained by either party. By putting the physical aspect of a relationship first, a couple will never survive the long-term relationship marriage requires. My educated guess is, this couple never planned or talked about their future, goals, expectations, or values. They never talked about who they are and what they need personally to survive and never had any spiritual consideration either. Clearly, it takes very little effort to give in to the emotion in the moment and physically jump in bed with someone.

Randy is a guy who will continue this pattern of behavior. He will no doubt have sexual encounters with many women who will fall into his web of impulsive behaviors until he reaches a point of grief and emptiness himself. Perhaps then, God can open his mind and heart. As we learn from this letter, Randy is a real person—someone who is truly lonely—trying to find love "in all the wrong places." His future looks destructive, and his heart is very deceived.

Becky is not without responsibilities in this relationship either. She was a willing recipient of what transpired. She also has no boundaries. With no foundational principles, the above list applies to her as well. At the time Randy came into her life, she was the same self-seeking person he was. Now she is left alone asking a serious why question, "I just don't know why there are horrible people in the world who do awful things and don't think they do anything wrong." Yet she was a willing participant! She was no different from the girlfriend who pulled into the garage and had sex with her husband.

You may be wondering why I say this since I have no facts to back it up. Well, I know human behavior, and I have seen this pattern repeated many times. *Needy people need people.* They don't view anything long term and do not see consequences down the road. Becky willingly grabbed onto Randy, and she took a hell of a ride (I mean that literally). When you latch onto a man with all the above problems and a man without anything to give from within and you are the same, emptiness has nothing to give. Two empty people = emptiness which Becky cries out saying, "I'm done with men"—empty and broken. She further says, "No one would want me anyway. I am ruined!"

Don't you, as a reader of this, want to reach in and hug this broken person? I do! I wish I could sit down with Becky and answer her why question. The pain of this is, she is a real person who is the mother of a real five-year-old little girl. Let's look at what possible hope awaits this five-year-old. I'll call her Julie.

Julie is a witness to some very dysfunctional behavior that blurs the lines of right and wrong, which causes her to feel insecure and be fearful of her future. She feels the loss of a father and is helpless to help her mother. Her life is totally out of control and, at five years old, is not equipped to handle any of this. She did not ask to be born into this situation.

She was born to be loved, nurtured, and cared for in the security of loving parents with strong values to impart to her to help her be strong against the evils of the world—teaching her to love and value herself so that when she is old enough to love and be loved, she will not fall prey to men like her father who are empty.

Sadly, with a mother who feels the way Becky does (*broken*, *empty*, and *ruined*), Julie has a very dark future. Once she starts school, she will look everywhere for value and acceptance. Without a foundation of love and values and with no God, the evils of the world will pull her in, and she will, most likely, end up worse off than her mother—as laid out in previous chapters—moving into sex, drugs, and substance abuse.

From only the information "Dear Annie" shares in this letter, I hope you see why divorce counseling and a strong co- parenting strategy are so necessary before entering into new relationships. The security and daily function of the child and or children *must take priority.*

According to Becky's letter, she consulted an attorney; and according to her, it is all his fault, and he ripped her off. The job of an attorney is to settle the case. Get the divorce legalized by dividing the assets, custody, and child support according to the laws of the state that has jurisdiction over him. He can try to overrule the law in some cases, but he must present evidence and arguments to override those laws, and they must be compelling enough to do that.

Let's just assume, in this case, Becky did not have compelling enough grounds to get everything she wanted to overrule the mind of the court—another strong reason why a couple must resolve major future decisions before ever consulting an attorney. Thus, divorce counseling is the best choice to make the right plan for the future of all concerned. (Less attorney time = less expense.)

Did Becky get ripped off by her attorney? The answer is "no!" An attorney charges what he charges and can only do what the law will allow him to do.

What Does a Good Co-Parenting Plan Look Like?

1. Parents must determine the division of all assets and figure out living arrangements for the welfare of the children and each other.

2. Decide if the children will reside with one parent or both parents jointly and how they share them—separate days or weekends?

3. Determine financial responsibility, child support, and/or spousal support.

4. When planning to move forward, agree to stay flexible.

5. Dissolve as much anger and resentment as possible prior to future interaction between the two of you.

6. Work toward peaceful interactions and smooth transitions.

7. Future relationships acquired by parents should not be introduced to the children until it is determined the relationship is heading toward becoming permanent, resulting in marriage.

8. Most importantly, the couple needs to understand change is a part of life, and, therefore, *negotiations never end.* Sometimes, circumstances arise that require both parties to be willing to come back to the table.

The numbered steps above are just a few suggestions to begin the process. Each couple has unique situations that make it impossible to address each possibility here. The idea is—try to exhaust all possible daily conflicts and solutions *before* they arise as areas of battle. My goal is to prepare couples to move forward with a "solution-oriented mentality" where *peace* is the desired result in all future interactions between both parties.

It is also important here to know children have a way of working with their parents to get what they want—when they want it. Since children will have divided homes with separate rules, it is very important for couples to have predetermined the *same* rules for each household experience. Maybe even the same responsibilities such as taking out the trash or making their bed as an example. These things should not change just because they are in another household.

Creating a stable environment with firm and loving support would be impossible to manipulate if his/her boundaries remain the same no matter where they lay their head. Each parent should be easily accessible to the child, and at no time should a child be made to feel alienated from either parent. When rules are different in each household, every time a child goes from one place to another, he/she must readjust. This is not what you want to do to your child. By agreeing as parents, the question you don't have to answer is, "Why do you make me do this when Mom never does?"

I can't stress the importance of implementing stable plans. As the children grow, school sports and outside activities must be considered by both parents regarding how and when each parent will be involved in those activities. When these possible conflicts are not discussed beforehand, unspoken expectations become heated disagreements, causing the child to assume enormous responsibility for the conflict, and you do *not* want to do this to your child. If this step is ignored as unimportant or unnecessary, our children will continue to face uncertainty and become victims of instability and frustration. Divorcing parents must not only commit to doing what is in the best interest of their children but also discuss expectations and possible future disagreements in advance. A good divorce counselor should cover this with you.

Perhaps this is a good place to talk about broken people. If you were moved like I was by Becky's *why* question, and you see Randy's obvious pain and frustration, don't you just want to reach in and pick up the pieces of their lives and try to put them back together? I do!

Does our God really care about individuals and their daily lives? Does He really know us so closely to see the mistakes we make? Is He really interested enough to give us answers to our daily struggles? Reading back over this "Dear Annie" letter, I am reminded of John chapter 4 and the story of the Samaritan woman at the well.

Jesus stopped off at a well in Samaria to get a drink of water. But was that really His mission? He is so aware of our every move and hears our every heart's cry. He knew the confusion of this fallen woman who really had a heart for God. Perhaps, like Becky, she had questions also. Her life was an embarrassment. She did not want to be seen by anyone, let alone a man like Jesus. He knew she would be at the well, and He felt her conviction and shame. She went late in the day for her daily water supply. She did not want to be mocked or ridiculed for her many obvious sins. But when Jesus asks her for water and then, as a stranger, begins to tell her everything about herself— having had five previous husbands, and the man she was living with now was not her husband—she was overwhelmed with the possibility that Jesus was either a prophet or could He be the promised Messiah she had heard about?

As He talked with her about her deepest concerns, which was about worship, she wanted desperately to know the one true God and how to worship Him and Him alone. Others had pointed to the hills and false man-made wooden gods placed on the highest point on the hillside. Her question was one we all have. "Where must I go and what must I do to find God?" To talk with Him and worship Him?

As I paraphrased from John 4:23, "Jesus let her know Truth. "She knew right away He was the promised Messiah. She was so impacted she dropped her water jug and ran into town to tell others. This simple, quiet, yet broken person was like Becky in our letter. She was ruined and empty. I am sure in her haste she no doubt dropped her clay jug, and the water spilled out of that broken vessel just as all of her sins spilled out for Jesus to see.

She left so unashamedly running into town, telling everyone who she had spoken with. We know from the book of Acts she was responsible for many coming to believe in Christ as the promised Messiah. Jesus, no doubt, tells her, "Go and sin no more." And because I like happy endings, I believe when she went home to the man she was living with, she did not continue to live in sin with him. No, I believe she told him who she had met; and I'd like to think that he believed also and was convicted in his heart, and they both committed their lives to each other in a public union celebration!

I believe Jesus, the Son of God, was at the well for her and that He went out of His way to meet her where she was. I believe this because Jesus said, "Go and sin no more." He knew the outcome of her commitment that afternoon. In His perfect timing, He knew her heart would receive Him, and she was ready for the Spirit of God to come into her heart and life so that she could worship Him in Spirit and in truth.

How about you, my reader? Are you ready to surrender your life to Jesus Christ—to allow Him to guide you and be in the director's chair of your future? Are you at a point of enough is enough? Looking for love in all the wrong places? Are you ready to give your family or yourself a different path to peace and forgiveness?

If you are, then surrender everything you are to Christ—lift it all up to Him to change your life forever. Just as He knew everything about the simple woman at the well, He already knows everything about you too. Receive Him as your Lord and Savior, and He will give you wisdom and strength to go forward and do the right thing for everyone in your life.

Why do I know this? Because, almost fifty years ago, I too was like the woman at the well, broken, searching, and wanting to know how to worship God and have a personal relationship with Him. I believe it is the cry of every heart. When we do this simple act of confessing our sin and receiving Jesus's love and forgiveness, John 1:12 (NIV) says, "Yet to all who did receive him, to those who believed in his name, he gave the right to become children of God."

I pray as you take this step, that your future becomes a better place than your past. Your next step is to tell someone who you know is also a believer and ask them to point you to a good Bible-teaching church near where you live.

Having taken this step, you may now become aware of new insights hidden throughout the remaining chapters. No, it will not be magic.

It will still take work, but as you progress, you will feel yourself get stronger as a person. Right now, you are at the starting point of the best journey of your life. I began my journey over fifty years ago and can testify that while it has not always been easy, it has been wonderful!

Chapter 3. What effective parenting looks like!

Classic illustration of a couple : What not to do.

1. Randy has no_____or structural_____.

2. No thought of_____consequences.

3. No_____of the family.

4. _____no_____.

5. Not_____by example.

6. No_____with God.

Randy fell into a pattern of seeking another before ending a relationship. No doubt he did this before with Becky. Either with a girlfriend or another wife.

7. Easy to conclude_____came before any foundational wisdom.

8. A couple will never_____long term
_____of marriage.

9. No_____or talk of_____,
_____or_____.

10. Becky is the same_____person. God designed women to be responders to men. Her_____and
_____were different from Randy's more long term.

11. Reason for Becky's hopelessness is she wanted a _____
and_____.

12. _____produces_____.Julie their five year old daughter has a very dark future.

Note to leader:

1. Go over list for good co-parenting plan on pages 40-43. Discuss with the group adding any other suggestions.

2. Also a good time to see if any in your group need Christ in their lives as the Samaritan woman did. Read or discuss her story and ask if any in your group feel as she did and would like to make

a new commitment to the Lord or commit to a deeper walk of obedience to His will?

Answers:

1. purpose, boundaries

2. long term

3. leadership

4. Selfish, goals

5. taught

6. connection

7. sexual union

8. survive, requirement

9. plans, future goals, expectations or values

10. impulsive, motives and expectations

11. future and security

12. Emptiness, brokenness

Chapter 4

How to Begin Again with Someone New!—Dating

The number one quality I wanted in my next husband was a close relationship with Jesus Christ. His life and values had to reflect not only a desire to live out his commitment, but I also wanted to see it demonstrated in his life.

Because this was my most important value in finding a partner, I sought out churches with adult singles groups. In Southern California, I found two very prominent singles groups. One was at Calvary Chapel in Costa Mesa, and the other was Crystal Cathedral in Orange, California. I attended both gatherings several times a month for almost three years before I met my husband, Dan. It took that long to finally meet the right person for me, and it was God's perfect timing for both of us.

We each had reached a point where we were tired of playing this dating game. Separately, we told God we were tired of going to meetings; and if He (God) desired for us to be alone for the rest of our lives, we were fine with that, believing God alone was enough for us to focus on. Miraculously, however, within a few weeks after that prayer, we met each other through a mutual friend; and within a few hours of conversation, we discovered we had both prayed the same prayer.

Our first date was amazing, talking into the wee hours in front of my home. I like to say we still would be sitting there if it had not been for both of us having to use the bathroom! When God brings couples together for His purpose, life becomes exciting; and within six months of our first date, we were married.

We combined three teenage children. Dan had a fifteen-year- old son, Kenny. I had a fourteen-year-old daughter, Melissa (soon to be fifteen on her next birthday), and my seventeen-year-old son, Chris, moved in with us after having stayed with his father until he graduated from high school in early February 1980.

Dan's son Kenny was rebellious right from the start. He was into drugs and took his dad's car on a joy ride, driving for two days with no license. We had him arrested and then placed on a boy's ranch for the remainder of the school year.

My daughter, Melissa, not wanting to return to her father's home, was a model student and obedient to our rules. My son Chris was going to start college in the fall and planned to lifeguard over the summer months. He took a job at the Hotel in Lake Arrowhead as a bell boy. Both of my children were compliant with our only two major rules:

1. Take care of your room.
2. Attend church on Sunday.

Along with being helpful with little responsibilities, Chris always took out the trash from the time he was eight, and Melissa often helped me with meals. Because my work schedule caused me to arrive home late, I usually had things ready for her to begin dinner for us. My children were happy to work as a team, and things ran smoother without Dan's son Ken.

However, from our wedding date in July to January of 1980, we had major adjustments to work through. Having no previous experience at blending two families, it was a work-in-progress. Each day was a new adventure, presenting new challenges. At times, various personalities would cause friction, and we all had to work together to solve issues as they arose. I am sure if you asked each of us the same questions, each person would remember it differently and have very different perspectives. Hopefully from the steps in this book, you will learn how to be better prepared and save your family from major setbacks.

Through the Full Gospel Business Men's Fellowship International, Dan and I met a couple who had just gotten married and were also working at blending a family. They each had a daughter from previous marriages but only one daughter lived full-time with them. Jim was an associate pastor for a church located in San Bernardino. He and his wife, Deby, had just gotten married about the same time as us; and because we had so much in common, there was an immediate connection. They invited us to come to their church and become involved, which we did; and after a month or so, we took over the divorced/singles ministry.

When we first started, the church already had over five hundred people and was growing rapidly. We were meeting in a vacant storefront that, due to the growth, we would soon move out of. Services were on Sunday and Thursday night, and our singles ministry met on Friday nights. The group started off with about 30 to 40 single people. These gatherings provided a safe place to meet and fellowship with other Christian singles in similar circumstances. The group consisted of some who never married, some who were divorced, and some who had lost their partner through death.

One of my favorite messages at the time was from Paul's second letter to Timothy, chapter 3, verses 1–8 (ESV), as I again paraphrased from my own memory. I titled the message "Creeps and Silly Woman in the Church." The passages read as follows,

> People will be lovers of self, lovers of money, proud, arrogant, ungrateful, unholy, heartless unappeasable, slanderous without self-control, brutal, treacherous heartless, swollen with conceit, lovers of pleasure rather than God, having the appearance of godliness, but denying its power. Avoid such people. For among them are those who creep into households and take *silly women* captive.
>
> Burdened with sins led astray by various passions, always learning and never able to arrive at the full knowledge of the truth. (emphasis mine)

Of course, my purpose was to motivate the women not to be like these silly women and the men to not be creeps as Paul described in this passage of scripture. Having attended other adult singles meetings, both Dan and I were well aware of similar individuals coming into the church. The following story is about three of these individuals and their outcomes.

Jackie was a very outgoing gal in our fellowship. She attended church almost every Sunday, was so happy when we started the singles ministry, and was always eager to help. I admired her because she had started a preschool from her home which enabled her to take care of her own two children while she also earned a good income. She had a strong work ethic, was resourceful, and divorced from her children's father.

The second person was *Jim* who, from all appearances, seemed to be a guy who had everything going for him. He drove a very nice vehicle, wore what appeared to be above-average clothing, and was polished and very gracious. He had his own business as a locksmith and was divorced several times.

The third person was *Gloria* who was a soft-spoken individual who was very closed. She had one daughter and was always at church when the doors were open.

All three attended our meetings, and at the time, as new leaders, we did not know anyone individual enough to be aware of developing relationships within the group. Our job was to bring people together in a setting of fellowship and biblical teaching, followed by us going to various coffee shops afterward to become better acquainted. From time to time, we would have retreats and fun outings up in the mountains above San Bernardino where we lived. Eventually, we were getting to know each member of our group.

One night, in the wee hours of the morning, I received a call awaking me from a sound sleep. The caller was Jackie. She was totally distraught and in between fits of crying and frustration. She proceeded to tell us she had just found out the guy she was dating had cheated on her.

After discerning the entirety of this situation, we learned, Jim was intimately involved not only with Jackie but also with Gloria, and while Jackie thought their relationship was exclusive, she was heartbroken to discover Jim had another within his reach. Jim is certainly free to date anyone he chooses, but discovering that he was intimate with both women broke Jackie's heart.

This situation created a problem for us to solve for which we notified our senior pastor to make him aware of the situation. He said he felt it was inappropriate for him to ban Jim from coming to church; however, we were free to ban him from our singles ministry.

At our next meeting the following Friday, Jim showed up with Gloria. When Dan asked to speak with Jim privately, he left the building, but Gloria decided to stay. We proceeded as normal, and afterward, everyone filed out of the room taking off in various directions until Dan, Gloria, and I were the only ones left in the room. In a few minutes, Jim came sauntering in to pick up Gloria. He appeared to be very angry—making a fist, he punched at my husband. Dan ducked while Gloria and I managed to decompress Jim's obvious rage and anger.

From that point on, he and Gloria continued to date.

Several months later, Jim came up to us after church and asked if he could talk with us in our home. After giving us a formal apology, Jim proceeded to tell us that he and Gloria had set a date to get married. Jim talked about their plans and then went on talking about his past marriages. Meanwhile, wanting to get some alone time with Gloria, I asked her to join me out on our deck.

When we were alone, I said, "Did you happen to notice the way Jim was referring to the past and his former wives?" It was troubling to my spirit that Jim was using the word "b———ch" a lot. Her reply was simply that she loved him and wanted to marry him. She also expressed her regard for Jackie but brushed it off as unimportant.

Jim came out to join us, and we said our goodbyes. It was difficult to give a blessing, but we were gracious and wished them well. Their wedding came off several weeks later, and we chose not to attend. We heard it was a grand affair complete with a helicopter takeoff from where the ceremony was performed.

Meanwhile, back at our singles ministry, another romance had been brewing with a new gentleman, *Chuck*, who started attending shortly after we had our confrontation with Jim. Chuck was immediately taken by Jackie. They seemed to hit it off right away. Because Jackie was working alongside us with refreshments and other various activities, we were able to give her some one- on-one time to help her sort through the pain and mistake she knew she had made. We offered her counsel that, hopefully, set her on the road to a better future.

Chuck had two children also, and as their romance blossomed, it soon became a union of lifetime love connection. Back then, we were just leaders, not ordained ministers, so Jackie asked if we would stand in with her at their wedding ceremony. Years later, we found out Jim and Gloria had a very bitter breakup, leaving Gloria far worse off than before Jim came into her life.

And, as far as we know, Chuck and Jackie are still together.

From this story, I am sure you can learn who was the Creep and which one turned out to be a silly woman and of course, last but not least, the one who became wiser than she was before, resulting in long-term blessing from God.

Remember the "Dear Annie" letter in chapter 3 about Becky and Randy who both appear to be unchurched? Unlike the *Silly Women* in 2 Timothy who were trying to find happiness in Creeps, Becky was more like the woman at the well—an empty vessel to be indeed pitied who needs compassion to bring her full circle. And Randy, the same. They both need supernatural transformations that only the touch of the love of Christ can bring. In conclusion, before beginning a new relationship, the big question one needs to ask themselves is: Am I ready? And a bigger consideration is: Are your children ready?

To determine readiness, a very important factor to evaluate is *your individual situation and circumstances.* God called us, first and foremost, to live a life of *peace* so couples need to observe the adjustment pattern of all family members. Ask yourself these three questions:

1. How smoothly is your past interaction with your former spouse going?

2. Are the financial arrangements and all elements of your total property settlement package falling into place?

3.   What, exactly, is your individual need for companionship?

Note. People often talk about looking for their "missing piece," but the truth is, they should already have all their pieces in place before setting out to find someone else with no missing pieces either. So take time to be completely healed before entering the dating scene.

When that time comes, it does not mean you throw caution to the wind and rush right out and move into circulation. From my experiences with singles and with myself, personally, I'd like to suggest a plan to follow:

—   **First**—Take a deep breath and make a list of what your responsibility was in the breakup of your past relationship. Hopefully, through counseling and dialogue with friends and family members, you can *face some of your own shortcomings.*

—   **Second**—Make a list of what others say are *your strengths and weaknesses.* Don't try to defend yourself or justify what they tell you, but rather, take an honest look at yourself. Sincerely work on the blind spots that need changing. Discover who you really are. If need be, take a personality class or explore an area of education or activity which you have always desired to do.

—   **Third**—make a list of at least **ten attributes** you would like to have in a lifelong partner. Here are just a *few to get you started*: characteristics such as a good communicator, open and freely expressive, generous with their money but wise, kind to others, good listener, sensitive and aware of those who are around them, and seeks other's interests above their own.

—   **Fourth**—Go over your list and determine if you, yourself, meet all the same standards and criteria you expect in others. Work on your own weaknesses and take a good look at changing the things you can reasonably change to be your **authentic self**. (What you see is what you get.)

- **Fifth**—After you complete your list, prioritize what's most important to the least important.
- **Sixth**—Make a list of goals you would like to achieve one year from now, two years, and so on up to as far as you want to go. Then determine how you can make them happen.

If you already have an established group of friends or people you work or fellowship with from your circles of activity, engage those closest to you in your goals and choices. Some of the best second marriages come from friends who know you best, introducing you to someone they know.

Above all, give yourself a lot of time to heal from the pain from your past relationship so you can begin to see people through a different lens because many tend to gravitate toward the same negative personality traits they just divorced (*e.g., People who divorce alcoholics often marry another alcoholic*). Be aware and watch for warning signs. The following is an example:

Before: You wanted the life of the party guy, joker, and storyteller, always laughing keeping everyone entertained. Now: Give the strong silent type a different look. The one who has some life but waits before he speaks. You may be surprised at what you find.

Along with all the above points, give yourself plenty of time; experience a number of different individuals, see them in all kinds of situations, and, above all, stay away from that which sends endorphins and dopamine to the brain that has a way of masquerading itself as *love* (which isn't) and blinds us from getting to know the *real person* we're with.

Instead, we who believe in God and have a moral code of ethics must never stop exercising self-control. As your author, I don't live in a vacuum. I am very much aware of how quickly we can fall prey to creeps. But when we choose to walk in obedience to God's will for our lives and not put ourselves in situations or settings where we become vulnerable to our weakness, we win!

Finally, dating opens up new challenges, new discoveries, and new restraints. While preparing for your future and watching for caution signs along the way, you can begin again with confidence to find success. Always include God in your plan and make sure you are looking for someone who is, without a doubt, "equally yoked" in the same solid beliefs as your own.

Chapter: 4. How to begin again with someone new!

DATING:

1. Explore your top qualities you want in a life long partner. Make a list.

2. Timothy chapter 3:1-8

    a. Men will be lovers of_____,_____,_____, _____

    _____,_____,_____, no_____, and

    so on the key character traits are lovers of_____and pleasure

    rather than_____.

3. A creep has the appearance of_____, but denies it's_____.

4. A silly woman is led astray by_____always_____ Never comes to the full knowledge of the_____.

5. After reading the illustration of the example given discuss possible character traits of each person. What do you see in each person.

    Jim:_____

    Gloria:_____

    Jackie:_____

    How closely does it seem to line up with the above

    scripture? Note to leader :

    We are looking for character qualities 2 Tim 3 tells us to avoid. And giving your group insight as to what to look for in a mate.

6. Do you personally or have you in the past displayed any of these Characteristics? You do not need to respond openly to your Group only if you feel it is a good thing for you to do to help Others.

    Need not give personal details.

7. Before beginning a new relationship: KEY QUESTIONS?

    Am I_____?

    Are my_____ready?

8. Steps to begin a new relationship:

    a. Face your_____. Make a list of your_____for the breakup of your past relationship.

    b. Based on the_____people in your life what do you see from their influence on your character as a _____and/or_____in yourself.

    c. Determine if you have the_____you desire.

    d. Prioritize your list of 10 things you want in your mate Number one being the most important to the least Important quality.

    e. Establish goals : one year from now. Two years and So on.Go up to 10 years. It helps to write each down.

9. Always include_____in your plans. Do you know His Will for your life.

ANSWERS :

1. 10

2. self, money, arrogant , ungrateful, unholy, heartless, no self control self and pleasure God.

3. Godliness, power

4. passion, learning, truth

7. ready, children

8   a. shortcomings, responsibilities

    b. quality, strength, weakness

    c. qualities

    e. One and so on to 10 years.

9. God

Chapter 5

Long-Term Relationships

Introducing children

U until now, you believe you have found the right person. Their qualities are comparable with your list of priorities and goals, and together, you have a strong connection, communication, agreement, and love. If all the above are in place, you might be ready to move into a *marriage commitment*.

This could be a good time to introduce your children (yours and his/hers) to the permanent place of blending two families and considering the many personalities in the mix. No longer is it just the interest of the couple. Combining multiple personalities, different ages, and different needs all must be talked through step by step.

All too often, couples just fall in love; and because they are in love with love, everyone wants a piece of that love including the combined children. They rush down to the minister or justice of peace and have a quick ceremony, and everyone is joyful, right? Then, real life begins. Reality starts moving into our daily lives, and, if this is your first experience, you are totally unprepared for any of it. Personally, I just thought that when Dan and I married, all the brokenness was now over; and we could all be happy together. Only in an ideal world does that really happen.

Instead, what really happened was that we faced tremendous daily challenges and situations; most were totally unprepared for, and depending on your anticipated abilities to handle transitional moments, those abilities will determine the outcome, going forward, long term. No matter the number of personalities involved, I hope you're beginning to see how important it is to work out some of these transitional emotions beforehand.

How Do We Do This?

If each person, coming from a previous marriage, worked through divorce counseling effectively, the process will be a smoother transition because husband and wife have been interworking with their previous partners and have leveled the playing field to where communication is freely transparent. The children coming into a new home together, with a new father/ mother team, will not feel emotionally betrayed by their natural parent, making the transition much more palatable. Open communication is so important, and if you have a good counseling partner in place, you will be ahead of possible conflicts.

Meeting the former spouse

When Dan and I taught our "Premarriage Classes for Blending a Family," we taught the importance of the meeting. Most of the couples we were involved with had no prior divorce counseling. For most of them, the interaction with their former partners was bitter or a battleground. Communication was strained and often ended in angry frustration!

"The meeting" is a very important step because the new husband/ wife coming into a relationship with stepchildren will make the parent of the children feel infringed upon. Filling them with unwanted resentment and if this is not handled properly will undermine the stability not only of the child/children but also of the new couple coming together.

In our class, we guided the couple blending their family to invite the former spouse to a public place for coffee or a meal. They could do this together, or the new wife could invite the former wife; or the new husband, the former husband. Either way, it is comfortable for all to do it initially.

At that meeting, after pleasantries are expressed, the new stepparent should begin by saying he/she is not coming into this new marriage to take the place of the former father/mother, but rather to partner with your new spouse X by carrying out the same rules, goals, and expectations he/she has for their child. Always be looking for transparent open communication and dialogue— whatever is necessary— to bring harmony to all parties.

Here is one example

We had a couple come to our class who were planning on blending their marriage with the wife's three children. The children were elementary school ages. The new husband was not previously a parent, but he was good with children. The couple was Elaine and Allen (fictitious names). Elaine was formerly married to Jack.

After we had taught on "The Meeting," Elaine contacted Jack, asking him if they could meet to talk about their children. Jack was very hostile on the phone. "Why do we need to talk about the kids? We have never agreed on anything in the past." After this opening confrontation, Elaine calmed him down, and "the meeting" was scheduled.

They met for dinner. Allen and Jack were meeting for the first time. Upon their greeting, he explained his plan to marry Elaine. He openly told Jack he had no other children, looking to partner with Jack to be a support to him working together carrying out Jack's plan for the future of his children. An amazing thing happened in the very next moment after that statement.

Jack, broken and humbled, began to cry! All battle shields were leveled, and he laid down his arms. From that moment on, Allen had made an inroad to open communication with Jack, explaining how much they had learned from our class. Jack became a willing father for transitional change. After Elaine and Allen married, Allen and Jack began parenting together. We have lost touch with them for that was almost twenty-five years ago. But I remember as they related this story of their first meeting how Elaine and Allen felt after their first encounter. Humility goes a long way when confronting hostility.

Other points to discuss at "the meeting" are as follows:

- Mutual goals for the children
- Education
- Spiritual considerations
- Each child's housing/living arrangements
- Financial considerations
- Children's financial needs

These are just a few items to get you started. Obviously, each situation is different, but these are basic things to start opening dialogue.

The third and fourth are often considerations couples never even discuss until they are in the final stages of combining their children. It is mind-boggling after talking with couples preparing for blending how little they discuss the financial considerations when coming together as a family. Life is going to be very sacrificial at this point! Blending a family can be an expensive undertaking, so your budget and expectations need to be considered.

We once counseled a couple who came to our premarriage class. Rose had a ten-year-old daughter, and Bill had no children. We came to the night where the course teaches on finance. Professionally, Bill was a dishwasher with no plans to change his career; so to provide more income, Rose was planning to leave her daughter with Bill and join the military.

By this time in our course of study, we had established open communication with this couple. In a private discussion, we were able to bring them to a point of awareness in their plans. Both could see this was not going to have a positive outcome for any foreseeable future. Rose contacted me the following morning, saying, "Bill and I decided not to marry." I was doing cartwheels over my entire living room. This might be a good place to discuss an awkward topic.

Knowing the evils of the world we are living in today, we want to be trusting of those we invite into our private space. Our home should be a safe place of protection from the outside world. Children's safety must always be our number one priority. As single parents, we can be very trusting of our circle of friends, family, extended family, and even church family, but let me be very candid here: Do not ever leave your children alone with anyone you are not fully acquainted with.

As an example, if someone from church is a tutor and wants to help your child with their studies by tutoring them, fine, great, but not alone in the child's room or while you are not there. Young children often become abused by molestation or even rape; you will never know what happened until you see a change in your child.

This even goes for the men you date and even the prospective stepfather of your children. Please exercise caution by not rushing into marriage. Knowing and seeing people in all circumstances is so important for the safety and security of your children. Just because a man goes to church or prays before a meal does not mean he is a *Christ follower* who walks in close fellowship with God.

Rose was going to join the military and walk away from her responsibility as a mother to protect her daughter. Truly, it does not take much to see where her ten-year-old might have ended up. So beware, be wise!

After planning the future arrangements for the protection and security of each of their children, a couple can now move into a position of marriage. By now, you will have introduced your children to each other and, depending on their ages, have agreed to prospective living arrangements.

This step is talking with your children about your plans and how they will fit into the plan, by assuring them of their continued involvement with their natural parent all following a joint agreement. "Train up a child in the way he should go and when he is old he will not depart from it" (Proverbs 22:6 NKJV).

When dealing with children, I have not personally done this, but I have seen it work, not in blended family situations but in a classroom. The process is a contract between the child and you as parents. The child is rewarded after fulfilling his/her contract— agreed-upon (age-appropriate) responsibilities and expectations that become a viable part of the family unit. If you desire to pull the former parents into the formulation of the contract, even better.

This contract is to be formulated with input from the child. The reward must be something the child totally wants and desires. Or it could be a special trip or getaway they have longed for. However, you draw up this contract, you as parents have to agree to it along with your child. Each party signs the agreement. And it is posted in the child's room.

The closest I ever came to doing this with my own children was when I was "potty training." I made a chart and found some stickers, a star for little potty and a bird for big potty. The stickers were rewards. When they achieved these steps and no longer had accidents, the great part was that they got to wear grownup underwear. Chris, my oldest, was two and a half by the time he accomplished his top reward of his underwear, and my daughter was two. They always say, "Girls don't take as long." The point, of course, is that it worked, and the beauty of it was that I did not have to get frustrated or angry with my child.

Likewise, the contract works the same way. Because the child is involved in the planning, his discipline becomes less confrontational. If the natural parent is also on board at the planning stage carrying out the same system at his/her home, then a child will develop strong cooperative skills. After all, is this not how all of life works? When you develop a skill, you agree to use your skill for a monetary reward or outcome. When that does not happen, you open yourself to being fired or moving to a lesser skill/smaller-reward job.

I have seen this work in a classroom setting; however, I know the transition to a secure loving home with a contract could prevent ongoing friction and unachieved expectations. Above all, we want to build self-worth and support for the success of our children.

The reward most definitely must be a desired item or want of the child. If they fail to meet the contractual agreement, discipline is so easy. You simply go over the contract again with the child, assuring them, if they follow through with the agreement, you will come forth with the reward. Then say, "How can we make this happen?" It levels the playing field. No one is the evil stepparent or the strict disciplinarian. It frees us to place responsibility directly on the child and their need to fulfill the agreement and gives reason for parents on both sides of the aisle to give plenty of hugs and lots of pats on the back.

It's so much better than shouting, humiliating, slamming doors, and crying. Not to say that will not happen occasionally, but a parent needs not to be the one doing those latter things. A child will only be angry at themselves for their own shortsightedness (not at you). At that point, you, as a parent, are the encourager, calmly reinforcing the child's agreement by telling them you can't wait until you can give them what they want.

Note. In the event of a teenager's *attitude* preventing them from being motivated by a *reasonable reward*, the contract may contain, instead, preagreed-upon privileges the teen would forfeit should they choose to be uncooperative. Their contract ties fair parameters to privileges so that when the teen *chooses* to ignore the agreed-on parameters, they also *chose* to give up privileges. It was *their choice. (No need to raise one's voice or get into a yelling match.)*

Here's a real-life example of one mother who was tired of yelling at her teenage daughter:

The teen was consistently late for school because she slept late and took too long *primping* herself in the bathroom. However, the agreement said, if she continued to be late to school, her bed would be removed from the room, and she would have to sleep on the floor *(which happened)*. If she still was late, she would lose her dresser drawers and stack her clothes on the floor *(also happened)*. If she still was late, she would lose her curling iron *(happened also)*, then her hairdryer *(happened)*. The best part was, there was **zero arguing**, and the *mother never had to raise her voice* with her daughter. It wasn't long until she got to school on time and earned back all the privileges she had *chosen* to be taken a way from her. *Contracts work!*

Above all, I cannot stress the importance of spending individual time with each child, doing what the child wants to do, not just tag along behind you and your new lover. Really zero in on your child or stepchild. It can be as simple as a walk with his/her dog, a drive to the store, or a fill-up at the gas station. It can even be a task as long as your attention remains focused on the child.

Discipline is another subject that's usually not addressed before marriage either. Although men usually assume this role, as parents and stepparents are concerned, take time to establish guidelines so the children *(and stepchildren)* of both marriages clearly understand the consequences of bad behavior.

My daughter once said to me, "*No* is a complete sentence." So often when we tell our children, "No," we feel a need to justify the *why* of that answer. This always leaves the door wide open for further negotiation or manipulation. More often the latter. Whatever you say to a child, you must be prepared to follow through with the statement to the end. Discipline must always mean what is said.

If you say, "If you don't settle down, I will throw you out the window," the window better be two feet up from the ground. Because you must never give a child an ultimatum without following through.

Always carry out any conditions you required. Doing so brings respect and obedience back to you. If you believe in spanking a child, it should be carried out by the natural parent (*not the stepparent*). For the most part from my own childhood, I was spanked for disrespect. Open defiance is not solved by sending a child to his room for a time out. I never got a spanking I did not deserve, but I never got very many either. Being the last child has some advantages as I watched my older siblings being spanked for justifiable behavior, and I learned not to do the same. I can count about five or six times I was really spanked.

While rules for your home need to be followed by everyone, the stepparent should always enforce what the birthparent decided is best for their child, which, by using the contract we discussed earlier, should make follow-through much easier.

My husband, Dan, came from a divorced home. His father was an alcoholic and, by hanging out in bars, found another woman. Dan and his brother were ten and seven when their parents divorced. His natural father rarely kept up his visitation with his sons.

It was not long after their divorce that Dan's mother met and married another man who said, while they were dating, he only had one child. After they were married, she learned he had a total of four children, and his mother lived with him. None of this was discussed or even acknowledged before their marriage.

It was not long into their marriage when Dan's mother became pregnant and had a son Rick. His stepfather had two older boys and a younger son and daughter. Dan's mother now had seven children. His stepfather was very kind to Dan's mother, and when she was around, he never displayed his dark side. When the older boys came home from school, he would stand them in a line and beat them with his belt. Sometime after Rick was born, his mother noticed the black and blue bruises on Dan's body. The next day after his stepfather went to work, she packed up Dan, Lee, and baby Rick and left. She was sad to leave the rest of the children but had no choice.

Note: Always flee insanity. This man had Jekyll and Hyde syndrome, and no one who does such unexplainable behaviors should be allowed to have access to or influence your children?

In Summary

Parents often reach the point when they sit back and look at how their children turned out under their ability to raise them or train them. Proverbs 22:6 says, "Train up a child in the way they should go." Our children are individuals! Each has his/ her own gifts and temperament. We, as parents, sometimes say of our adult children, "I don't know why he turned out the way he did because I treated each child the same."

When raising children, all levels are not equal. The needs of each individual child may be extremely different in all aspects— financially, physically, spiritually, and mentally. I say this because it is impossible to keep everything even. One may have musical talent and need lessons and instruments while another finds his nose in a book more satisfying. As a parent, you may spend more money on one child than another. It is not written that each child gets the same amount of compensation. Parents are often guilted into thinking they must treat each child equally. One may need medical attention and so forth.

The important thing is, by celebrating each child's individual talent, the resentment issue will not arise. Each child should be made to feel special, and their gifts and talents are what God has placed in them. They must be nurtured and encouraged differently. Therefore, training up a child in the way he should go does not pertain just to spiritual growth. Our children are three- dimensional beings—*physical, intellectual, and spiritual*. It's our job to "train them up" in all three.

In the next chapter, I will discuss the roles of a husband and wife, how it works in a blended family, and how to do things "God's way," which can affect the outcome of generations to come.

I can't stress enough the "call to peace." Our home environment must be a shelter from the outside evil of our unsaved world. The home must be a place of *peace* and *love* and *a soft place to fall*. It's a place where voices are discussing and interacting with each other because there's the freedom to say what's in your heart. That's how God intended it to be.

Chapter:5

LONG-TERM RELATIONSHIPS: HOW DO WE ACHIEVE IT?

1. Determine how_____the_____Is working with your former spouse. Is there open_____.

2. "The_____" a very important step.

3. It is important for the parent of the child/children form a workable_____with the new _____.

4. The purpose of the meeting is to_____a_____ parenting plan for the needs of child/children going forward.

5. Desired place for "The Meeting" is_____.

6. Be specific about_____needs.

7. _____is the most important consideration for your children. Be_____and be_____.

8. _____as a united group with children about the entire_____ going forward. To ensure no misunderstandings.

9. Individual_____a must.

10. Step-parent_____rights and privileges set by the parents of children.

LEADER: Discuss with your group the summary of chapter 5. Open with. "Did you discover a new understanding of Proverbs 22:6 (Train up a child…) after reading the summary?

ANSWERS:

1. effectively, transition, communication

2. meeting

3. Relationship, step-parent

4. Establish, consistent

5. Public place

6. Financial

7. Safety, be aware, wise

8. Talk, plans

9. time

10. reinforces

Chapter 6

The Role of the Husband

In today's blended family, the roles are no different from how God planned them to be in the beginning. The only addition to the original roles is the degree to which each party remains in contact with their children's father/mother. Contact with their former spouse must and should always include their new partner. Not doing so opens yourself up to suspicion that can create jealousy in your new relationship. Therefore, transparency must be the most important element.

Ephesians 5:2 says, as I paraphrase, "Walk in love, as Christ also has loved us, and hath given himself for us." The previous chapter laid out a plan for everyone to be on board for the new marriage to be effective. While this chapter's focus is on the new couple coming together in marriage with children from their former relationships, I just want us to focus on *the couple*.

When a couple first gets married, without children in the mix, they have time to grow closer together before adding new personalities. A newly married couple in a blended family is very different because of the added personalities. It is very important for the new couple to have their own private space; therefore, boundaries must be set for the children of this new family. The ages of the children must also be considered when forming your plan. Not only does the couple need privacy, but the children do also.

My daughter was almost fifteen when I married Dan. Dan's son was also fifteen and soon to be sixteen at the time. It was important each child have their own private space. Our home's main living space had the master bedroom with its own private bath. On the same floor, we had a second bedroom for my daughter Melissa. She had her own bathroom, which was the main bathroom of the home. Our third bedroom was downstairs from the main living space where Dan's son, Ken, also had his own bathroom. When children are the ages ours were, every consideration must be in place to ensure proper boundaries and privacy are accounted for including proper locks on all doors.

My career took me away from home for long hours, and Dan had local employment in real estate. His hours were very flexible, enabling him to be home when the children got home from school. It was important to me that Ken and Melissa were never left alone together. That problem settled itself when Ken took his father's car on a two-day joy ride, which caused him to spend the rest of his school year on a boy's ranch. It's not the way I would have wanted it but the way it turned out.

Establishing private spaces ensures respect for each person's peace of mind. It is not uncommon for stepchildren to sometimes become infatuated with each other. That said, every effort must be made to create respect and boundaries. A father's role as protect or needs to be taught to his sons as well.

Inspiration for the role of the husband and wife came from *A Biblical Portrait of Marriage.*

Protector

Let's begin here as the first responsibility of the husband in his new role as a husband in a blended family is that of protector. God is our Heavenly Father. He protects us every day as His children.

Most of His protection is unseen by us against our enemy, the god of this world whose evil demonic forces are at work against us. In the same way, a husband protects his wife and his children by standing between them and the outside world. He does the physical things to make sure his home is secure. He puts the proper security in place with locks and protection from predators and outside elements and makes sure the home is warm and dry.

More than physical, a protector has the courage to come between an aggressive person trying to cause harm or abuse to a member of his family. He has the wisdom and forethought to see danger long before it happens. When he plans his way, he incorporates preventive measures for danger and/or unforeseen emergencies.

Adam was made in the image and likeness of God. This protective quality is in man's DNA, and it's important for a father to instruct his sons to be protectors of their wives and women in general. Eve came out of Adam. She was created from Adam's rib. God fashioned her to meet every need Adam had for companionship—body, mind, and spirit. When he saw her for the first time, Adam said, "Bone of my Bones and Flesh of my Flesh." His instinct was to protect her, making sure nothing would harm her, knowing he was responsible for her welfare.

Some theological views have said that when Eve was deceived by Satan, Adam knew the consequences of her sin. He believed in God when he was told death would be the result of eating the fruit of that tree. He walked daily with the Lord. Can you imagine what they must have talked about before Eve was even thought of? Adam was so confident in his relationship with the Lord he did not want to be without Eve. He knew, after she ate of the fruit, that she was going to die; and even though he knew it was wrong to do so, Adam chose to eat the fruit with her because he did not want to live without her. Adam was a type of Christ—a protector of his wife even if it meant death.

From that image, we can see a husband and father of his family must be completely dedicated to meeting the needs of his family by protecting them from every possible intrusion into their sanctuary of space.

Remember Randy and Becky, the couple from the "Dear Annie" letter in chapter 3? Randy is a perfect example of a man who completely lacked understanding of how the husband and father protector role works. His leaving Becky and their daughter alone by running away from all responsibilities to have an affair with a woman he brought back to his and Becky's garage for the night shows no strength of character or protective qualities. Adding to his betrayal, he brought his five-year-old daughter right into the middle of this affair; giving her no protection from the unrestrained discipline of this new woman is nothing but disgraceful. A man like Randy is void of self-control and lives totally in the moment, but *a real man protects his children.*

Most marriages fail, in my opinion, because of broken people. Broken people come together, seeking to be repaired by other broken people. Much of this brokenness stems from broken children, raised with bad role models in broken homes themselves. Sadly, this is not how our Creator intended the family unit to function. Thankfully, there is a way to stop the cycle and turn it around.

I know of only one *master repair shop* that specializes in broken families and relationships comprised of broken people. Through submitting to the Master of the shop and giving oneself over to His way (not ours), a man can learn how to become the protector of his wife and children.

When we humbly place ourselves in the Master Repairer's hands, He shows us how to die daily to our selfish desires and desire instead to live out the will and purpose of God. When a man does this, it is amazing how the desires of the flesh become bridled (contained). A major fruit of being controlled by God's Spirit is self-control. As I paraphrase 2 Timothy 1:7, Jesus said, "By their fruit you shall know them."

Provider

The second responsibility of the man is to be the provider for his wife and family. God's pattern of men being the provider has gotten lost in our society today. Indeed, many marriages begin with both the husband and wife having prosperous careers. Both are educated, and both are providing. The compensation varies by responsibility given to career and professionalism attached to each other's job descriptions. Because many of our millennials come from single-parent homes or blended families, they seek to be both independent and financially independent. Therefore, it brings distortion into a marriage and to a blended family.

One of the major conflicts in a marriage relationship happens to be finances. When a wife works outside the home, she makes choices based on her work-related responsibilities. Often. these choices conflict with the personal needs of the new family life.

These conflicts often create resentments and frustrations because of undiscussed expectations and assumptions. In a household, when two career-minded adults come together in a blended family, the minor children often get lost in the mix. The care and protection of these children must be the primary consideration to ensure peace of mind. Proper supervision for minor school-aged children must be in place when both parents have careers.

When I was age six, my mother taught school. My sister was eleven, and my brothers were teenagers in high school. My sister and I walked home for lunch in every kind of weather. She fixed lunch for the two of us, and then we walked back to school together. It was a daily event that happened over seventy years ago. Times are very different now. Most children remain in school until three in the afternoon or later. This does allow for children to be supervised.

In my understanding during the COVID crisis in our country, one of the good things that has come from it is that employers have found many of their professionals do better working from home. Setting them up with a workspace at home has ended commute time and makes for a more-relaxed worker. Production has not diminished at all either. This has allowed children to return home to a safe environment and protection. Many of those companies have continued this new work ethic.

A couple planning to marry must consider their individual careers and how the time will affect the daily lives of each person living in the household. Sharing the workload and developing a rhythm creates harmony in the home. To avoid conflict, one key element is communication. Taking time to plan a daily/weekly/ monthly schedule, including the children's activities after school, keeps harmony in the home. No one in a family or blended family can be totally independent—living on their own schedule. This is one of the reasons second marriages with children fail. If you are too independent, perhaps getting into a blended family situation is not something you should consider.

Blessed are the flexible, for they will bend and not be broken!

The reason I said all of this is that if a couple wants to follow the instructions given to us by the author of marriage and family, the husband/father must be the primary provider of the family. Financial responsibility rests on the shoulders of the husband. If it takes the combined incomes of both husband and wife to meet all the expenses, be sure everything is discussed and agreed upon *before you marry*. To get you started thinking in the right direction, there are concerns that have a caution sign posted on them as follows:

- Child support payments
- Household expenses
- Clothing for all
- Emergency funds
- Car care (both if two)
- Food
- Housing
- Travel
- Vacation time and funding

When we taught this in our class, we told our couples that Dan and I found that keeping separate accounts of his funds and mine never worked for us. We worked from one joint account. We both knew what and where the money was going each month. The list of above items had to be covered before any personal items were bought individually. We agreed not to make any purchases costing more than a certain amount without the other knowing why and for what purpose.

When a couple has separate careers and feels justified to spend their earnings independently, it causes conflict. You have heard it said by one spouse, "What is mine is yours," and the other spouse says, "What is mine is mine!" I'm here to tell you— *that will never work*. If you can budget a portion from each income source for personal expenses, no questions asked; do so, knowing you both have freedom with agreed-upon boundaries. As an example, a savings account could be set up for each, and a percentage of each person's income could go there on every payday for individual wants and/or needs of a personal nature. This prevents conflict and the feeling you must ask permission like a child and prevents resentment from building between couples.

In a future chapter, I will cover blended families from couples with adult children coming together combining adult married children and grandchildren. This is a very different financial picture, and often, both the husband and the wife have strong individual financial independence—very different consideration with no minor children in the home. The most important part of this discussion of provider and provisions is that God has given the husband final authority, knowing that he is responsible to carry the full weight of that decision and will take an extra job or whatever to fill in the needs of the entire family if necessary. "The husband is the head of his wife just as Christ is the head of the church and gave His life for it" (Ephesians 5:22–23; paraphrased).

Leader

The husband is also the leader of his home. No one would begin a road trip without a destination point. Indeed, everything we do in life has a plan, a goal, or an outcome built into the design. If I had to point to the reason why most marriages and families fall apart, the number one reason would be families traveling down the highway of life with no destination in sight.

The children are asking, "Are we there yet?" The parents have the car in drive—everyone is moving but with no clue where they will end up. Is it any wonder why marriages fall prey to boredom and lose momentum? Couples move into daily routines and fall into bed exhausted for no real apparent reason.

The responsibility of the husband is to *lead his family*. He is the one who devises a plan and sets goals to bring excitement and adventure to his home. He teaches values for his children to follow. He also takes the lead spiritually, for he is the priest of the household.

As a leader, he and his wife must teach their children together and involve themselves in helping people in need within their community, caring for an elderly family member, or taking care of someone's pet. He plans family activities and fun things to look forward to. He is the one who takes the wheel of his family and the one who they can depend on to get them out of difficult situations.

As the priest of the home, a husband/father needs to be the one who prays with his children, reads Bible stories, points them to depend on God, teaches them about finances and the importance of giving and saving, makes church and worship a major commitment every Sunday, and plans fun family time. Leadership is vital to the life of any family.

Selfless love

A husband must, above it all, love his family and his wife more than himself. This love is the same kind of love Christ (the creator of everything we see) had when He gave Himself to die for us. It is interesting here in the roles between a husband and wife. A husband is commanded to love his wife. If he obeys this command the way it is intended, the wife can easily fulfill her role to submit to her husband.

When God created a woman, He created within her a natural desire to submit to her husband's leadership. When a husband is a leader, protector, provider, lover, and priest of his home, a wife, who was made to respond, can easily take her place under the husband, a place where she can freely become the submissive person she was meant to be. A leader knows when and how to direct his household. A leader has a plan that considers the will and mind of each member of his household. He makes sure everyone is on board.

When men fail to take this responsibility, disrespect usually follows. It can begin with the wife who takes over these responsibilities, then rebellion results from everyone because no plan is in place to follow— no structure.

In my generation, fathers were providers only, coming home from work, taking their easy chair for the rest of the night. Mothers ran the household. From where I sat, she did it all: washing, ironing, cooking, gardening, cleaning, and shopping. As a child, my siblings and I pitched in and helped, going off to play when our chores were finished. When I watch American families today, it seems like no one is at home. Everyone is off in a different direction, and very few families eat together at onetime. We have a lot of work to do to bring it back to the way God designed it.

A man is responsible to lead his family. He has the final say and shoulders all the responsibility. Are you, as a man, willing to take the wheel of your life and family, creating a plan and guiding and directing their lives according to the map God has provided? It takes oceans of love and patience, but God promised help when He said, "I will draw near to those who draw near to me" (James 4:8 NKJV; paraphrased).

Chapter 6: THE ROLE OF HUSBAND IN A BLENDED FAMILY.

1. All contact with former spouse requires_____so _____or_____is not the outcome in your new relationship.

2. Challenges in a blended family:

    a. Many_____.

    b. Setting_____.

    c. Creating_____for_____.

3.. A husband is a_____of his family_____ and_____. He would lay down his_____for his family.

4. Husband_____for the family even in a blended family.

5. Organize a_____,_____,_____plan.

6. Keep_____in_____ _____.

7. Organize a_____of all combined finances, however primary needs of the household must be come from_____.

8. Being a leader requires a_____.

    a. Teaches_____.

    b. Plans_____.

    c. Guides_____.

9. Husband_____for his family in their presence as well As in personal prayer time.

10. Must_____his family. A_____of God.

Note to leader: Assign a planning session with the men in your group to come back next time with a plan in place. Have them share how or what reaction and impact this step had on their family. Positive/ Negative.

Answers:

1. transparency, suspicion, jealousy.

2. a. personalities

   b. boundaries

   c. own space , children

3. protector, physically, emotionally, life

4. primary provider

5. daily, weekly, monthly

6. finances, one account.

7. budget, the husband

8. destination

   a. values

   b. activities

   c. responsibilities

9. prays

10. love, command

Chapter 7

The Role of the Wife

Beginning in Genesis chapter 1, as I see it in most versions, God creates a man from the dust of the earth and breathes into him the breath of life. In verse 26, "Let us create a man in our image," indicating a pluralistic God, consisting of a Father, Son, and Holy Spirit. We see here that Adam was alone with his Creator for some time before Eve was created. In chapter 2, God looks at Adam and says, "I will make for you a helper." After God creates all the animals and provides a means for Adam to work and care for the garden, He realizes none of the animals issuitable as a companion for Adam. So He causes a deep sleep to fall upon Adam and removes a rib from his body and fashions Eve to perfectly fit the design of Adam's body, enabling them to reproduce offspring and future generations.

God then took Eve to Adam who was so taken by her beauty. He stated, "This is now bone of my bone and flesh of my flesh I shall call her woman." From these simple beginning verses, we can see a woman's primary role is to be a man's helper.

God designed a woman from a bone next to the most valuable part of Adam's anatomy, the heart. The heart is an organ that literally supplies life to our bodies. As a helper, in that same physical sense, a wife is a life-sustaining help to her husband. She helps him fulfill his purpose. She is the driving energy behind his motivation. Success loses fulfillment and purpose without a helper behind a man. That's why God told Adam it was not good for him to be alone.

Today, career-minded women have distorted this role. Men grow up confused when many of their mothers, either out of necessity or divorce, have taken on the role of leader and provider of their homes. Consequently, growing up in broken homes or in homes where both parents are working has caused men to expect their women to take over much of their role. Women, likewise, are not taught (or shown how) to be helpers but rather to be self-sufficient just in case you are left with all the responsibilities. Men have abdicated their roles as providers, leaders, and protectors of their families.

If I had to cite one reason for the breakdown of the family unit, I would put at the top of the list that men have not been taught (or shown) how to be leaders/providers. It's most often because they have come from broken homes where their parental examples were poor providers. Teaching young men to have a strong work ethic and giving to others during their growing up years are essential to the maturity of men. Helping a neighbor or friend in need is a great way to build these skills.

As women, our primary role is to be a *helper*, but because of the above-stated problem in our families, women have no *leaders*. Most of the time because we have no leaders, we step into a marriage partnership and begin telling our husbands how we will help them.

An often-overlooked verse in scripture is 1 Peter 3 (paraphrased), concerning an unbelieving husband. The instruction tells a woman to, "Fit in well with her husband's plans in order to win him to Christ." I would like to state this is what a *helper* also does in the wife's role. She fits in well with her husband's plans whether or not he is a believer. However, the plan should be the road map of the husband. Now I am not saying daily a man lays out a plan, but I am saying that he is the one in control. He guides and directs his family.

Most companies begin with a business plan. It begins with perhaps a product, and then by doing a business plan, the desire or need for the product is determined. Then a production plan is put in place to determine the production based on the need for the product. After that, the company hires people to meet their production goals and distribution of the product. Behind all this, there must be a leader. There must be someone who sees the end from the beginning and can guide and direct the process. A family must also have similar leadership.

A wife can only fit in with her husband's plans when he is a leader with a plan. She can only be a strong helper if her husband will lovingly instruct her how to help. So before a couple marries, the wife should ask her husband, "How can I best help you?"

A Well Thought-Out Plan

1. Structure

When dealing with a remarriage situation, the husband and his *helper* should begin by structuring a plan with each family member in mind, discussing all aspects of their home. The helper then can fit in well with her husband's plans. A good leader is sensitive to the nature and well-being of each member of his new family as well as his wife. This is not to say a wife has no authority to state or negotiate her desires. I am by no means indicating dictatorship here. A couple cannot be a couple unless they walk in agreement. I am assuming by this time you have come together in agreement on the family's primary considerations, financially, spiritually, physically, and emotionally.

Harmony cannot take place unless these issues have total agreement.

2. Goals

Before we begin, we need to see where we are going to end up. Having something new to look forward to should include everyone's hopes and ambitions—career goals for both husband and wife (if she also has a professional career). Keep in mind the need for flexibility and adjustments along the way. Nothing can really be permanently planned, but it's enough so there are no surprises along the way. We cannot know the future, but we can prepare by having a cushion in place such as extra savings or a backup plan. Goals may only be hoped for things; always open for negotiations and change.

3. Children's future needs

It is difficult for me to address this concisely, not knowing the ages or circumstances of your situation. However, a plan must bein place for each of your children's futures.

Note. The following steps are merely foundational and are often structured as the family grows together.

The key purpose of this discussion is to point out the importance of a plan. To establish how she can best help, a helper needs to fit into a plan. Her offer should be in the form of a question, *"How can I best help you?"* not as a statement, *"This is how I will help you."* The proper question promotes a leadership response. Perhaps the best way we, as women, can encourage leadership in our husbands is by coming underneath his lead and encouraging him to plan.

Note. When a husband is a Godly leader, provider, protector, priest, and lover of his wife and family, it makes the wife's role much easier.

The second role for a wife is to "submit to her husband as she does to the Lord" (Ephesians 5:22). This one has gotten a bad *rap*. Many men have taken it to mean they can just do anything they want to, and the wife is less than a servant under the authority of her husband.

First of all, notice a wife is not commanded to love her husband. But the husband is! Why is that? God made woman from man. She is a very part of him. She is made from a part of his body, so she is a **natural responder** to his affection. It is built into her DNA to respond to every need her husband has. But if a man deals harshly with his wife, she does not know how to respond to this.

One of the reasons why women fall prey to *battered wife syndrome* is that the heart of almost every woman is to bring peace to a situation. This is not to say some women don't exhibit mental issues and have been known to batter their husbands. This is a rare occurrence, but it does exist in our society today. Since Dan and I started this journey with marriage and premarriage counseling, we have encountered this several times, and it must be handled the same way—by moving to a safe environment, along with the children (if necessary). Women can suffer from Jekyll and Hyde syndrome just as well. As stated previously—flee insanity!

Worth repeating. When a husband is walking in his role, as lover/leader, a woman has very little difficulty submitting. A man is commanded to love in the same way as Christ loves His church—a self-denial type of love. When he is a loving leader, loving provider, loving protector, and a loving forgiving priest, how could a woman not respond to that kind of headship? Both are to take up their cross daily and live a self- denial existence. The rewards are great in this type of environment. If a man does this, he should have a submissive wife who responds to his love, making him a very happy man.

With regard to a woman's natural desire to respond to her husband, it has been said, "A man who complains about his wife *is telling on himself.*" Except for mental or emotional illness, a man who understands his wife's built-in response mechanism realizes it is to his advantage to be considerate of his wife's needs.

If both of you have gotten through these last two chapters without conflict, fully understanding your roles, you may be ready to blend your families. A happy home must have strength at the top. At once, your home should be functional. When past relationships have been worked through, a plan is in place with proper boundaries, and you each have a clear picture of your roles, success is in your future. I am going to close this chapter with an important lesson from Genesis 20:1–16, involving Abraham and Sarah. Abraham feared the king of the southern region because his wife, Sarah, was very beautiful, and he thought the king would have him killed to take Sarah as his wife. So he told the king that Sarah was his sister. It was partly true as Sarah was his half-sister. It is apparent from this passage Sarah submitted to what Abraham told the king and, not knowing Sarah was Abraham's wife, Sarah was taken from Abraham to be prepared for the king.

One could raise a question here and say, "Why didn't Sarah say something in protest?" Because when a wife submits to her husband as she does to the Lord, her trust is in a much higher authority than her husband. God is our ultimate protector. In this story, God intervened on Sarah's behalf. God appeared to the king in a dream and told him Sarah was Abraham's wife.

When we, as believers, trust in the Lord, we can be sure He will intervene when our husband makes mistakes. As wives, we are submitting not only to our husband but also to God. Since submission is a command from God, when we walk in obedience, we can count on God's intervention even when our husband fails.

I could write several chapters on this subject from personal experience. For example, there were many times when Dan and I made tough financial decisions or career changes, which altered our security, yet God continued to provide for us. Never once were we without shelter or food in our bellies. Our trust must be always in God.

Chapter 7: ROLE OF THE WIFE

1. The primary role of the wife is_____.

2. If you have no_____how will a wife_____?

3. _____was created before the_____.

4. Wives are to_____in well with the_____of the husband.

5. A_____has a_____.

6. A leader is sensitive to the needs of_____family member.

7. _____family needs to be considered in the plan.

    a. _____support.

    b. _____issues.

    c. _____family, grandparents, etc.

8. Establish_____.

    a. _____for both husband and wife determine the effects it has on the routine of the family schedules.

    b. Family_____where you want to be one_____, five years and so on.

    c. _____needs of each child.

9. The second role of the wife is to_____.

    a. She submits to a_____leader.

    b. She trusts and submits to_____.

10. God is our ultimate_____,_____,and _____of all of our needs.

ANSWERS:

1. helper

2. leader, help.

3. Man, woman

4. fit, plans

5. leader, plan

6. each
7. Extended
   a. Financial
   b. Co-parenting
   c. Extended
8. goals
   a. Career goals
   b. goals, year
   c. Individual
9. submit
   a. loving
   b. God
10. provider, protector, supplier

Chapter 8

Remarriage of Empty Nesters

Couples with adult children, who have either lost a partner by death or divorce, present a new dynamic to the blended family. Their children are adults, on their own, and no longer living with their parents. These couples are somewhere between their late forties to retirement age, and the mistake these couples often make is the assumption that the children will be totally happy for them, taking for granted their future will be void of family resentments and problems. After all, we are all adults, right? Oh, how I wish this were true.

As much as we hope our children would understand, the loyalty and their protective nature kick in the moment wedding plans are even mentioned. After that, depending on how financially well- off the couple coming together is, the children's thoughts begin to wonder about what effect this might have on their inheritance after the death of one of the two persons getting married.

There are variations of this last equation, depending on the child's level of independence and their own individual financial success. Spoken or not spoken, adult children assume a lot. By nature, we are very selfish; and when parental loyalty kicks in, it can really create unexpected issues.

Years ago, when I was a manufacturer representative, traveling the entire states of California, Arizona, and Nevada, one of my store owners fell prey to cancer. Both Bill and June were in their early fifties. They started their Christian bookstore on a shoestring, but it was not long before it was turning a very nice profit. For years, they worked the store together and, sometimes, included their children in the family business. As their children grew up and married, they sought lives of their own, leaving Bill and June to continue working their business together. It was apparent they loved each other very much, and the news of June having cancer was not easy to bear. When they told me her prognosis was not good, and her time was not expected to be very long, I could not with hold my emotions.

Being the lovely Christian couple they were and dependent on the Lord for their future, they continued their daily life as usual. When the time came for June's departure, the family drew close together. They pitched in and did whatever was necessary to help their dad.

As a strong Christian family, they moved on, and Bill managed the store alone. I serviced the store several times a year, and I would see him at the various trade shows where he also purchased products from me for his inventory. It was at one of our annual conventions where Bill showed up with a new friend in his life. Ruby and Bill had met at the church he attended. They had known each other for a while now, and Bill told me of his plans to marry her. Indeed, congratulations were in order. They seemed very happy together, and several months later, Dan and I received an announcement of their marriage. We were both very happy for them.

As the months turned, so did the lack of peace in Bill and Ruby's marriage. Both sets of adult children were very unhappy with this new marriage. The children argued collectively and individually over the breakdown of inheritance and business-related affairs. When there were family gatherings or time spent with each other, it was a constant on-going discussion about their interest in their parent's affairs. For those of us who knew Bill and June, this was tragic for us to watch. Because of the interference from their adult children, Bill and Ruby's marriage lasted less than two years. Both went to seek a divorce, holding hands on their way into court. I can only imagine the pain they must have suffered.

I have no idea what the details were that led to this tragedy, but my instincts tell me that had the details been all worked out before the marriage union took place, Bill and Ruby would still be married today. If only they had worked with a counselor and/ or legal authority regarding the children's concerns, the problem could have been resolved, or, if not, the remarriage would not have taken place.

Dan and I worked in the funeral business for several years. Our position dealt with preplanning your funeral arrangements and having everything in place before death occurs. In talking with many couples, we found it difficult to even get couples to discuss the final process. Indeed, that was the most upsetting part of our job. It was as if they thought if they talked about the process, it would happen sooner! So the longer I put it off, the better. Dan and I have all of our plans in place from the time we were in our late forties. We did not draw up a will until we moved into our final home and retired.

Most of the companies where Dan was employed had life insurance policies for both of us, and we did not ever, in our married life, have a large enough estate to do an extensive plan. We both worked hard all our lives, but most of what we have to leave behind is our home and personal valuables. So we have stated in a will how those things should be dispersed among our combined children and grandchildren. Let me repeat what is written in the bible, "All of us are appointed once to die." Not one of us is going to get out of here alive unless we are raptured out with the Lord's return. That said, please put your affairs in order and preplan.

Marriages with adult children become difficult when the couple has their children scattered over the United States and beyond. It is often difficult to have consistent time together. Therefore, when a relationship develops, often it is totally void of input from outside family until marriage is the desired outcome. When marriage is brought to light, it is almost a shock to adult children. It is totally out of their realm of thought process. "Does Mom or Dad actually date at this age?" For some reason, children can't wrap their heads around a need for companionship after a certain age.

Adjusting to this kind of change is sometimes overwhelming for adult children, plus the assumption that they will even like this new intruder into their lives. Children will compare the lost loved one to the personality of the new parent. If they do not measure up, the behind-the-scene conversations begin, and depending on the degree of dissatisfaction among the players can create many problems. To stay on top of this, there needs to be open communication with each child, plus extended family members are very important during the courtship stage of a relationship. The couple's ability to foresee problems ahead and having a plan in place will make sure they will not be blindsided when the problem arises. Here are just a few subjects to tackle before marriage:

Division of estate planning

- Retirement pension plans
- Housing—his house or hers or selling both for a new
- Combining financial incomes and combined estates from former spouses

Breaking up the family home can be traumatic to some adult children. Personal family memories can be attached to material things in each of these homes. Family photos, happy times, and things children want to continue to share and talk about with their children. These things are worth preserving. Yes, even in divorce, children continue to remember warm memories of their growing-up years.

Recently, I put together my memoirs. My daughter and I had been estranged for over ten years. I thought about my own divorce and the ages they were when the divorce occurred. They were teens and pre-teens at the time and had lost touch with when we were a happy family. Their father and I were together almost seventeen years as stated earlier. The last five years were the difficult years. As I thought about this, I began to write about how their father and I met and fell in love. The happy memories flowed from my pen and developed into twenty-three chapters up to my daughter's birth. I still have better positive things to write about. However, I stopped to pen this book. The miracle of writing my memoirs was the healing of my family. My son called me and wanted to meet me in Pennsylvania for a trip down memory lane. He wanted to see where he was born and his grandparent's homes and where his father and I met and fell in love. We had a wonderful trip, going together to all of these places.

My daughter did not contact me until Christmas 3 years ago, and though she did not say why the sudden change occurred, she wanted to reestablish our relationship. I believe it was because I wrote these thoughts down on paper, causing her to realize how much she was really loved and how much her parents once loved each other.

Today, both of my children are adults in their late fifties and sixties. Their children are also adults. Pain from divorce or even death leaves scars that we sometimes have trouble healing. There might be a thin layer of skin over the opening, but a word, a thought, or action can quickly break it open. I believe God laid the need on my heart to write my memoirs. Maybe as a couple, your adult children need healing as well. Perhaps putting together thoughts, photos, or personal things can bring healing to past hurts and reflections. Doing these things can often help as well before you plan or introduce a new relationship to your adult children.

It is very important to finish your past before you start something new. While we may think our children are adults, in many ways, we hang on to threads of our past. Open dialogue with your children will go a long way toward healing.

I began this chapter with Bill and June and June's death and Bill's remarriage to Ruby. As stated, I have no idea what caused the final demise of their relationship, but I suspect the above list of possible considerations could be the *why* in their relationship.

Dan and I live in a very large retirement community. The last couple, Dick and Shaun, who we had the privilege of uniting in marriage, both had lost their former partners through death.

Shaun and Duane lived in the same development where we purchased our new home. We met at the pool one day and became instant friends. They wanted to know where we attended church, so we picked them up the following Sunday for services at our church. From that time on, we were very close friends. They were what Floridians call snowbirds. They were only here nine months out of the year and spent the summer months in a place up north they called home.

Several years had passed when Duane told us he had just been diagnosed with cancer. The prognosis was by no means a positive one. We were heartbroken, but because of our combined strong faith, we committed his life to God and trusted Him for the outcome. It was a battle to the end, and we were there in his final moments watching him leave us to go to be with his Creator. Duane's suffering was over, and peace could be felt by us all.

Shaun was in her early seventies and had no intention of finding a new partner. She had a fulltime position with an agency, placing traveling nurses all across the United States. She worked from home, which was convenient for her to stay busy and plugged in to life. She said, "I have no intention of getting married again." We remained friends as she adjusted to single life, traveling back and forth between Lake Michigan and Florida.

Years went by as they seem to do quickly now that we are retired. One day, when Dan and I were in California, I received a text from Shaun that said, "Met someone on the square."

I texted her back, "Marriage in the plans?" Her response was, "More when I see you."

When we returned home in late March of that year, we learned Shaun had met Dick. His story was even more traumatic. He and his wife of over fifty years had purchased a new home in our retirement community. They were here to close on their new home. They had gone to Home Depot for some items and were traveling on the highway when a young girl who was texting and driving hit their car head-on, killing Dick's wife instantly. Dick, as I recall, was uninjured at the time of impact. However, the loss he suffered in an instant was beyond a bodily impact. In that instant, fifty-plus years came to an abrupt ending.

After putting his life back together, he faced some very big difficult decisions for himself. He was in his early eighties and still physically in good health and full of life. After his time of grief came to a close, he realized—after living fifty years with a companion, he did not want to spend the remainder of his life alone.

While I do not know Dick well, I see him as a very practical person. No doubt for most of his life he handled traumatic situations head-on. He does not strike me as a person who stays down on his luck for very long. He assessed his circumstances and saw the wonderful years he and his first wife and their two daughters had together. While very sad, he decided to not stay in the place of despair yet; it was almost a year later when he and Shaun met.

Both sets of children had individual concerns regarding this new union. Shaun's children seemed most concerned for their mother's safety and well-being while Dick's children were still in grief over the abrupt loss of their mother. One daughter wanted Dick to wait at least one full year. However, Dick said, "What am I waiting for?"

When we arrived back home from our travels, wedding plans were in motion. A date was set, and we were included in their plans. Dan performed their wedding ceremony, and I stood in for Shaun. It's been over four years since they tied the knot, and everyone is still on board with it. The union has been good for everyone.

I still remember picking Shaun up on her wedding day. She was so happy. She asked me a question, "Why does this feel so much better than my first marriage?" As if the reason for her asking was because she was filled with a combination of guilt and joy.

My answer was simple. When we marry in the autumn/ winter years of our lives, we are usually in a state of peace and contentment. Our first marriages are very futuristic in nature, always wondering when the next thing happens in our lives, depending on how young we are. When we finish school, when the children come, when we settle in our first home, when... when...when. But in the final stage of life, you are living in the now. Every day is just being filled with the joy of living. It is not dependent on anything or anyone.

Fortunately, both Dick and Shaun are very comfortable financially. They both individually planned their lives well in their former relationships. Although they have never indicated conflict over these affairs, from general observations, I can see that the children from both sides are comfortable with their relationship. I also think they all have even grown to love each other.

Peace and love are a place of grace,
contentment with life as it comes moment by
moment.
This is the goal and hope for all late-life marriages.

CHAPTER: 8. Remarriage OF EMPTY NESTERS!

1. Major mistake these couples make is believing their children will be_____for them!

2. _____and_____nature kicks in the moment wedding plans are mentioned.

3. Depending on how financially solvent the couple is the question _____of comes into play.

4. Steps to avoid unforeseen problems.

   a. Consider_____of the children.

   b. _____concerns.

   c. Consult a_____or_____advisor.

   d. _____all children in your estate Planning decisions.

5. Selling and going thru the_____can be a difficult experience for the adult children.

6. Preserve family_____and valuables.

7. Map out each_____and form a _____ agreement.

8. Having a well thought out_____plan in place will avoid_____emotions.

9. _____and_____are the outcome late life marriages.

ANSWERS:

1. happy

2. Legality, protective.

3. inheritance

4. a. loyalty

   b. Financial

   c. counselor, legal

   d. Include

5. family home

6. memorabilia

7. estate, legal

8. distribution, painful

9. Peace, love

Chapter 9

Rooted in Dysfunction

When we allow God to take hold of our life, our future will never be what we thought it would be. Observers of my life have said, "You and Dan have done so many things in your life, so many different jobs and transitions. How did you ever do it?"

Now that we are in the winter season of our lives, looking back, we can now see it was the Master Director who most often shifted the gears, taking the wheel and turning it in an unexpected direction. Such was the case in 1984. Dan was finishing up law school in Fullerton, and my profession as a manufacturer sales representative had come to a close. Because I was the primary provider at the time, it was a real shock to the budget. But God always makes a way.

Through various avenues of ministry, Dan and I found out about a conference on "Dysfunctional Families." I heard about it while listening to the Christian radio station in my car and signed both of us up to attend.

Kathleen Case, from Christ-Centered Counseling, was the key speaker. She often filled in on the radio for Rich Buhler's program, *Talk from the Heart*. I had never seen her in person, and she had no idea who I was.

We showed up at the conference on the following Saturday. We took our assigned seats and notebook. About halfway through the conference, there was a question-and-answer time. Many of us had questions. However, we were both singled out from the audience and told Kathleen wanted to speak with us after the conference. We had no idea what was in store for us or why.

When the conference was over, we stayed to talk with Kathleen. She approached us, took my hand, and said, "You two are very special people." She continued, desiring to know if I was working and expressing her need for an assistant administrator. She asked if I could come to her office the following Monday to discuss it. I agreed to be there first thing Monday morning.

I share this little miracle with you because as we move through our lives, God's intervention is often missed. There I was in an audience of hundreds of people, never met this speaker before this very day, and she singled me out of the entire group. She turned to my husband and also asked him what he was doing. He explained he was soon to graduate from law school, and he would be studying for the bar. She said she needed someone to follow-up on some of her billing problems and felt Dan could work that out and earn some money while he was preparing for his law bar. The following week, both of us began working for her. (I will later refer to this story at the end of this chapter.)

As Kathleen's assistant, my responsibilities included designing the materials given to those who attended her seminars. This involved typing all documents and even putting the script into a document form. The front cover was inserted into the front ofa notebook, and the pages were inserted inside. I worked very closely with Kathleen; we became very good friends, and through her, I learned so much about family dysfunction.

We all come from dysfunctional families. Not one family can boast they were the perfect family. Looking from the outside in, to most of our neighbors and friends, we only see the best of what was projected to us. For the most part, people keep their lives in the privacy of their homes and behind closed doors.

Through the work I did with *Christ-Centered Counseling* and working with Kathleen, personally, I learned most families have a scapegoat. This person is the one who is blamed for all of the family's problems. They are the one who does not conform to the rhythm of the family and are usually in the middle of it all. They could be transparent or a behind-the-scene person, but because they are not the center of attention, they are oftentimes blamed for it all.

A good example of this from scripture is Joseph. Joseph was openly favored by his father mostly because he was the firstborn of Jacob and Rachel, who Jacob loved more than Leah. After Jacob worked for seven years in exchange for him marrying Rachel, who he was in love with, his father-in-law tricked Jacob into marrying his eldest daughter, Leah, instead. This deception resulted in Jacob having to work for Laban another seven years to acquire Rachel's hand in marriage. Nevertheless, Jacob was honorable and respectful of Laban, his father-in-law, and remained obedient until he obtained the bride he loved.

During those additional seven years, Leah gave birth to many sons of Jacob. She knew Jacob did not love her in the same way as he loved Rachel. She was the older sister who was perhaps not as appealing or attractive as Rachel. Their union was arranged by Laban who must have seen this as Leah's only chance for some degree of happiness. She knew Jacob loved Rachel, but God blessed her with many children in whom she found happiness and love.

During those seven years, when Leah was having her sons, I am sure she sensed that Jacob longingly desired to marry Rachel which, I assume, made Leah feel unloved in her marriage of convenience to Jacob. But by centering her affection on her children, Leah was grateful to be able to have a family. The account of this story can be found in Genesis chapter 37 to the end of Genesis. It continues with Jacob working seven more years and, finally, marrying Leah's younger sister Rachel whom he loved. Jacob and Rachel had a son they named Joseph who, because he was born to him in his old age by Rachel whom he loved, was favored over his older brothers who were jealous of Joseph.

One day, when Joseph was seventeen, he was tending his father's sheep when his brothers allowed their jealousy to take over their minds, and they plotted to sell Joseph into slavery and create a deception, changing the entire course of Joseph's life.

Can you see the dysfunctional structure taking form from the deception of Laban to the conception of Joseph? The children, no doubt, witnessed overwhelming joy from Jacob when he was finally given the privilege of marrying Rachel whom he loved plus the joy when she became pregnant with Joseph. You see, feelings inside a family unit are hard to hide. Even small children pick up when they are not favored more than others.

God blessed Leah with more children, but Jacob favored Rachel's children so much more. This dysfunctional behavior created a very high degree of jealousy among the rest of the children.

All through scripture, we can find dysfunctional examples. Adam and Eve's children were no exception. Cain hated Able because he seemed to be favored more by God. The reality here is, God looks on our hearts and the level to which we obey Him. Cain did not obey God and chose his own sacrifice, which was unacceptable to God (dysfunctional).

From the beginning of creation, when mankind was made perfect in the image and likeness of God, they were given the best possible future in their garden so perfect. Adam was told one thing to avoid. "But of the tree of the knowledge of good and evil you shall not eat, for in the day that you eat of it you shall surely die" (Genesis 2:17 ESV). And Adam passed that command on to Eve.

Adam did not need faith to believe in God. He walked with God and talked with God every day. He knew God personally. I believe it is safe to say Adam loved God also. As discussed previously, Adam knew the consequences of eating the fruit would cause death. In his defense, however, Adam had never seen death in the perfect garden— he didn't know what it was or the implications it caused.

Until Eve was created, Adam had not been tempted to ever eat the fruit of the tree. It was not until Eve was deceived by Satan that Adam disobeyed God.

I once took a Bible class in which the instructor posed this question to be answered for our next meeting. "Which is more important, faith or obedience?" We were also asked to have scriptural reasons for our answer. As I struggled with the answer to this question, my answer was **obedience.** All through scripture, we see "by faith" it was…!

By no means is faith unimportant. "Without faith, it is impossible to please God." Because of Abraham's faith, it was counted to him as righteousness, and it's the same for each one of us who believes. However, faith without obedience is dead. Obedience is the action of our belief or faith. It is the tangible proof that we actually do believe.

If our children constantly told us they loved us but constantly disobeyed us, what proof would we really have of their confession? Paul, in his letters, as well as other disciples in their letters, constantly spoke of obedience to the Word. Paul said, "Should we sin more so more grace should abound?" God forbids! We must display obedience in our choices and actions.

Jesus put it very plainly, "By their fruit ye shall know them." What is clearly displayed requires no judgment. In fact, in our own words, we have commented, "What you see is what you get."

A leopard does not change its spots! While faith is a necessary ingredient, obedience is far more important.

Because we are all rooted in dysfunction, for "All of us have sinned and fall short of God's glory" (Romans 3:23; paraphrased), our only hope for a functioning future is through faith and obedience to God.

My sincere hope for you, as the reader of this book, is that you will take these biblical keys and apply them to the future of your families. Most importantly, you transform yourselves by believing in Christ as your personal Savior and Lord, admitting you have fallen short of His glory, and have chosen to obey His will and purpose for your lives going forward by placing your future into God's capable hands and continuing to grow spiritually by studying His Word (the Bible). The best way to do this is by finding a Bible-believing church where the Bible is taught verse by verse and chapter by chapter.

The best advice I can give you on how to find a church is simple. If you can fit in by leaving your Bible at home and not taking it with you to church, "keep on searching!" The best pastors are those who teach what God says, line upon line where we hear what God says is the truth as it is written and not some manor woman's opinion. God's Word never returns void and, after memorizing it, comes to your mind repeatedly.

We are indeed rooted in dysfunction, but "God" is in the life-transformation business. He has been knocking on the door of people's hearts because He wants none to perish. He wants us all to be a member of His family and heirs of His kingdom yet to come. Embrace His love and become His child by faith in His death and resurrection that satisfied God's requirement for our sin problem to be "removed from us as far as the east is from the west and remembered no more." Take what you have learned here and change what has been dysfunctional to functional. Live a life of peace and love.

Remember, I told you about the moment when my husband and I were picked out of a large audience to meet with the conference speaker? Once you become a child of God, you will be taken in many directions. Sometimes, it will not be obvious. Life has many transitional moments, so be willing to step out of your comfort zones. I had never been an "assistant administrator" before in my entire life. In fact, I had to get a book telling me what my qualifications should be to take that job. I was overwhelmed by what I read and felt totally unqualified. But God! He knew my qualifications, and He equipped me for the position that lasted less than a year. I will never forget being called into Kathleen's office and told how much she appreciated me and had grown very fond of me, but she had just found out that she had cancer and did not have very long to live. It was a shock.

At the time, I asked God what was that all for. Such a short amount of time for what? It wasn't until thirty years later that I knew the answer. It was to learn what I did from Kathleen about dysfunctional families and to understand why Jesus said, "Perfect people don't need a Savior!" His ministry was meant for those who knew they were imperfect, sick, and dysfunctional and that they were incapable of making things right on their own.

From the beginning of the fall of mankind, God had a plan for our lives—to take us from dysfunctional to functional—knowing we could not do it without Him. On your journey, if you are seeking to follow God and be obedient to His Word that tells us to live, you should be able to look back over the transitions in your life and see how they were guided, supernaturally, by the invisible hand of God.

Have a great ride!

There are many biblical keys scattered throughout this book. Many are quite obvious, while others are here for you to seek out. They may be shown as important, major, or they may be contained in the scriptures themselves.

CHAPTER 9: ROOTED IN DISFUNCTION

1. After reflection on your past transitions in your life share with your group.

2. What biblical character do you most relate to and why?

3. After reading this book how has it increased your understanding and perspective toward remarriage?

    a. Toward either getting into a new marriage or your marriage now.

    b. Do you now have a deeper grasp of how your children are impacted by divorce and step-parenting?

    c. How the choices we make can change the entire dynamics of the family unit including extended family?

4. Either with your group or marriage partner discuss how you will apply what you have learned.

NOTE TO LEADER: The dynamic of each group will be different. Made up of couples getting married and blending families or those who are already married and want to stay married with a better understanding. You as a leader may also target singles who are just in the dating stage of a relationship. Adult children even marrying for the first time could have been raised in a blended family and now dating someone with an original parenting couple. Th ere are so many areas this book can be targeted and knowledge given to the attending class.

Do not just limit your target groups to blended families. Expand your understanding of how far-reaching this topic is

References

A Biblical Portrait of Marriage. Wilkinson, Bruce H., Dr. 2001, 2008.
   Walk Thru the Bible.

English Standard Version, ESV Text Edition. 2001. Crossway Bibles.

New International Version. 1999. Holman Bible Publishers.

New King James Version. 1979, 1980, 1982, 1990.
Thomas Nelson Inc.

About The Author

Dottie Klein graduated from Wisdom for Life school of Ministry with honors. She and her husband have served many years in ministry. Dottie is a grandmother to eighteen grandchildren and a great-grandmother to nineteen, and her love for God through Christ our Lord has been a continual journey.

www.ingramcontent.com/pod-product-compliance
Lightning Source LLC
Chambersburg PA
CBHW051221120626
46547CB00013B/1454